ONE

HOW **MALE ALLIES** SUPPORT **WOMEN**
FOR **GENDER EQUALITY**

ONE

HOW **MALE ALLIES** SUPPORT **WOMEN** FOR **GENDER EQUALITY**

Strategies, Ideas, and Stories
for Leaders to **Partner Together**

JULIE KRATZ

Niche Pressworks

INDIANAPOLIS

ONE

ISBN-13: 978-1-946533-18-0

For permission to reprint portions of this content or to purchase in bulk, please contact Julie at Julie@NextPivotPoint.com.

Published by Niche Pressworks; http://NichePressworks.com

ACKNOWLEDGEMENTS

This book was written in partnership with men and women leaders across the country who donated their time and expertise. We are thankful for the stories, ideas, and strategies benefiting gender equality. Their full interviews, bios, and pictures are featured on our website at NextPivotPoint.com.

Aaron Coleman	John Harkey
Brad Johnson	Josh Levs
Bryce Scanlan	JT O'Donnell
Carrie Kass	Karen Katlin
Chris Reap	Kim Graham-Lee
Dan Ingram	Kim Saxton
Dave Meeker	Kristin Kasselman
David Smith	Laszlo Syrop
Diane McDowell	Mark Jewell
Dolly Chugh	Michael Kimmel
Elaine Bedel	Mike Bensi
Eric Anderson	Mike Sale
Erin Albert	Nate Turner
Jack Powell	Neal Sengupta
Jen Marshall	Rachana Bhide
Jen Handley	Sebastian Rodriguez
Jeff Ton	Shauna Oswald
Jim Miller	Steven Szalay

CONTENTS

SECTION ONE:
WE ARE ONE

INTRODUCTION

Why It's Important to Involve Men

In working with successful leaders throughout my career and in our research, there is a clear and integral role for us all helping each other. For some reason, we rarely recognize the male allies behind successful females. This book is intended to help women understand the importance of men, and provide strategies, tools, and ideas for both to partner together for gender equality. Male allies are represented across a variety of roles – sponsors, mentors, coaches, advisors, managers, and advocates. They are men who support women as equals, believing in equal pay and opportunities.

From our research, we believe feminism failed to produce results because it was negatively perceived as "man hating" (ignoring 50% of the population in its cause). Now is the time to showcase examples of what "good" looks like and include men in creating positive change. Many of the men we interviewed told us small things make a big difference. From business leaders, to those in academia, to executive leaders, bestselling authors, and TEDTalk speakers, we have interviewed dozens of extraordinary men who have done extraordinary things to support women. They are truly one with the movement – as allies – alongside us, united to create positive change *with* women, not *for* them. Our book's title, ONE, emphasizes this shift from men vs. women, to a partnership where allies benefit equally from one another's successes. Allies aligning on common goals and speaking a common language.

In this book, you will find a simple set of strategies, tools, and ideas for partnering together. This is not a tug of war; it's not a zero sum game. We all stand to benefit when we welcome men into the conversation. Women are not going to solve this problem alone. We need the support of men to win together. And, as we found in our research, there are benefits for both. It's a win-win. We are ONE.

This is Personal

For me, this is personal. Ever since I was a young girl, I have believed in gender equality. Growing up in the suburbs of the Midwest in the 1980s, I enjoyed competing with boys, refused to conform to gender norms of risk aversion and weakness, and I believed women should have equal rights with men. Later, at Ohio State in the early 2000s, I minored in Women's Studies, learning about the gender biases holding us back. I remember reading books in our curriculum and feeling discouraged.

What were we supposed to do about this problem? If women were underrepresented in leadership roles, on boards, and with their pay, what role did we have in creating positive change? I remember men sitting in our classes checking the box to get the diversity credit, not participating, and mocking the content in the hallways. We may have thought we were including them, but forcing them to take the class promoted compliance, not support.

Entering the construction industry post Ohio State, I was the only female in a leadership rotational program at a Fortune 50 company ... and surrounded by 11 men. I was treated fairly, yet it was the subtle things, I now realize, that held me back. While my male peers were supportive, women often questioned my motives and dissuaded me from doing the "men's work." I remember sitting down with the highest ranking woman in the company (a vice-president) and asking her what she would recommend for advancement in the firm. Her reply? "Forget you are a woman." That was crushing to me as I tried to find my way.

I had the lowest starting salary because I didn't know how to negotiate as my male peers did. They brokered their first promotions. I did not. I was the last of my class to be promoted despite higher performance ratings. Why? I did not ask for a promotion. Yet, even with the barriers early in my career, there were several male leaders who saw something in me, took me under their wing, and helped me successfully navigate through six areas of the organization and two promotions in four years. They coached me, mentored me, sponsored me, and – most importantly – believed in me. One of my male allies told me, during my performance review, he wanted to work for me someday. He boosted my confidence more than he will ever know.

When I pursued my MBA at Indiana University (IU), I was once again in the minority. Only a quarter of our class were women. I led our professional development group and focused efforts on recruiting more females to the program. We discovered women, even a few years into their careers, had declined relocating for a job if it meant hurting their husband's chances. I was discouraged, yet cautiously optimistic seeing all these amazing female leaders in my class.

A pivotal moment came during one summer at IU. Working as a brand management intern at a Fortune 500 company, our class lunched with the CEO. I was nervous, yet excited, until he said, "It is difficult to promote women in the child bearing years." The sad thing is, I did not think anything of it until HR did an investigation on the CEO. I thought, "At least he is being honest about it." The gender biases we subconsciously associate with mothers is real. He was stating what we all think – is she going to be committed once she has a child? Will she want to stay at home or work part-time? Needless to say, I did not accept the offer to return full-time. Not with an openly non-inclusive culture. Now, nine years later, their performance and diversity numbers remain low.

The last phase of my corporate career was in consulting, primarily in agriculture. Talk about male-dominated! In rooms of all white men age 50+, I was treated as their daughter, even though I was the lead on the strategic plan or facilitating leadership development for the team. Yet, in this male-dominated arena, I found my calling. Again, I had a few male allies who saw something in me I did not see in myself. These leaders helped me become who I am today. One hired a coach to help me become a better coach and leader myself, another took a chance on me for my first coaching gig, and a third helped me land my first big sale at the company. Having men support me propelled my career and helped me start my business. As I train women to be successful leaders and build winning plans for success, I often reflect on the men who helped me get here.

Undoubtedly, my most important male ally is my husband, Rustin. A stay-at-home dad, self-proclaimed "manny," and my biggest fan, he is "all in." Without him, our business and family life would not be possible. Rustin maintains our home, takes excellent care of our amazing girls, helps with our business, and is always there when I need a nudge or to vent about travel snafus. He's our family's rock. In fact, when I originally took this book idea to him, I had the gumption to call it *Man Champions*. Rustin dismissed it flatly and coined, *ONE*, which better speaks to the inclusivity of the new women's movement (one needing men's involvement). He was completely right about *ONE*. Without him steering me, I would have moved in the wrong direction. He's my guard rails. Rustin keeps me and our family grounded and focused. We're lucky to have him. When I think about a male ally, he's the personification of one. Rustin proudly celebrates my accomplishments, supports his family in and out of the home, raises our children by showing them what "good" looks like, and instills confidence in the women in his life. I've never felt a power struggle with him. He's let me be the strong person I have always been, giving me the freedom to be my authentic self. He wouldn't want it any other way.

I would be remiss not to share the impact my late father, Dale, had on my life. While he was not the ultimate male ally, he supported me when I was a young girl. I remember my dad laughing with me, encouraging me to travel, and challenging me to be my best self. He loved me. He believed in me. He supported me. While I do not think he knew what to do with me once I was fully self-sufficient, he did not stand in my way. He let me be who I am. I am grateful for his support and for letting me succeed on my own merits.

Think about your interests for gender equality. The road has been a long one, a journey beginning 150+ years ago. And since the birth and rebirth of feminism, the statistics remain stagnant.

Statistics are not Improving

According to Catalyst's March 2017 report, women account for:[1]

- 5.6% of CEOs
- 19.5% of Board seats

---

[1] "Women in S&P 500 Companies," last modified June 14, 2017, http://www.catalyst.org/knowledge/women-sp-500-companies.

When I share these data with leaders, I often hear, "Be patient, it's changing." Yet, when we reflect on the journey of feminism, the statistics remain stagnant. According to the Pew Research Center, women in 2007 accounted for:[2]

- 2.4% of CEOs
- 14.8% of Board seats

The U.S. Congress Joint Economic Committee says women will not balance men in pay for equal work until 2059.[3] And, according to HeforShe (a UN based organization supporting male allyship), gender equality in the workplace will not be achieved until 2095.[4] We still earn 83% of the salary of men in similar roles doing similar work.[5] Rather than voice frustration at these slowly changing statistics, let's have a voice in promoting positive change together utilizing the tools in this book. Let's leverage strategies from experts and leaders who have promoted females or have achieved success as women. Based on our interviews when writing this book, we confirmed common traits associated with successful women: they engage men in their career development as mentors and sponsors, speak up for what they want, and draw clear boundaries between their personal and professional lives.

According to *Harvard Business Review*, women are 54% less likely than men to have a sponsor.[6] That's because men in leadership roles seek to promote those resembling themselves. In Joan C. Williams' book *What Works for Women at Work*, she outlines four key biases: the maternal wall, the tightrope, prove it again, and the tug of war.[7] She suggests the statistics for women are not

---

[2]   "Women and Leadership," last modified January 14, 2015, http://www.pewsocialtrends.org /2015/01/14/chapter-1-women-in-leadership/.

[3]   "Report: Gender Pay Inequality -- Consequences for Women, Families and the Economy," last modified April 8, 2016, https://www.jec.senate.gov/public/index.cfm/democrats/ reports?ID=76D42E65-B2F6-4370-9BCB-BA8FA1FD8EA4.

[4]   "Take Action," last modified 2016, http://www.heforshe.org/en/take-action/work.

[5]   " The Narrowing, but Persistent, Gender Gap in Pay," last modified April 3, 2017, http://www.pewresearch.org/fact-tank/2017/04/03/gender-pay-gap-facts/.

[6]   Berhane, "Why Women Need Career Sponsors More Than Mentors," https://www.fastcompany.com/3050430/why-women-need-career-sponsors-more-than-mentors.

[7]   Williams, What Works for Women at Work, xiv.

changing because of the subtle impact these key prejudices have on females in organizations. In my opinion, almost everyone has these thoughts:

- The maternal wall – If she has another baby, she won't want the promotion.
- The tightrope – She's so aggressive, she needs to tone it down or people will think she is a bitch.
- Prove it again – She did it once, but can she really do it again? Maybe it was a fluke.
- Tug of war – There are only so many seats for women at the table. I don't want them stealing attention from me.

Women are just as guilty of making these assumptions. We do it subconsciously. We limit each other, which is why having male mentors, sponsors, and inclusive managers is key to success. Curious about my own bias, I took the free online Implicit Association Test (IAT) available at https://implicit.harvard.edu/implicit/.[8] The results indicated I have little to no gender bias, yet in our research with our advocates, we found many admitting to biases towards both genders. For example, we judge men based on potential and expect them to take risks, where we often question females who are not the primary caretaker of their children, exude too much confidence, or act aggressively. Successful women challenge these unconscious biases, and they do so in partnership with men.

What is a Male Ally?

The *Harvard Business Review* article "The Men Who Mentor Women," outlines four key areas where men support females (for gender equality) by:[9]

- Using their authority to push workplace culture toward gender equality.
- Thinking of gender inclusiveness as part of effective talent management.
- Providing gender-aware mentoring and coaching.
- Practicing other-focused leadership, not self-focused leadership.

---

[8]   "Project Implicit," last modified 2011, https://implicit.harvard.edu/implicit/.

[9]   Valerio and Sawyer, "The Men Who Mentor Women," https://hbr.org/2016/12/the-men-who-mentor-women.

Based on our research, we would add another bullet point we will cover in section five – men as fathers and prioritizing fatherhood in partnership with motherhood. We talked to dozens of male leaders and public champions of women. When asked about their personal backgrounds and the origin of their passion, trends emerged. The stories had many commonalities including: a woman inspiring them at a young age, daughters they want treated fairly, and a genuine belief that being more inclusive is the right thing to do.

Many did not believe other men would exclude females or choose not to support this cause. They think every man is like them because they are likely in social circles with like-minded people. When I share this belief with women, they scoff, "I wish all men were like that." These male allies are more powerful and rare than they realize.

In early 2017, we found people preferred either the term "male ally" or no differentiating name at all for these men. Many commented it's human and the right thing to do. Calling these men out is like admitting equality is non-inclusive. Again, the perception of like-mindedness emerged: "Everyone is like me," and "Everyone is supportive of this." If only the statistics were changing. Clearly, not everyone is on board. As we socialized the term "male allies" with gender equality experts, their recommendation overwhelmingly pointed to labeling these men. In fact, research points to one clear factor encouraging more men to join in – recognition. They want to know how they can support us, and when they *do*, they want to know the impact. This reinforces the positive behavior, leading to more male allyship.

One of our experts, Dolly, NYU professor and author, weighed in on the challenge of any label to describe men supporting women.

> "Allyship requires risking something, not just declaring ourselves as allies. Even if it is just comfort, it requires risking something. One school of thought is none of us can declare ourselves to be allies. Only the people we claim to be allies for can describe us as allies. It's in their eyes. Allyship is in the eye of the beholder, not the declarer."

Let's call out these supportive men. It is less impactful when men use the term to describe themselves. We found the term male ally resonates because of its definition. Allies are defined as "dominant group members who work to end prejudice in their personal and professional lives, and relinquish social privileges conferred by their group status through their support of non-dominant groups."[10] It signifies we're in this together, side by side, a clear need articulated by the experts we interviewed.

At Pivot Point, we're advocating for a call to action – The Male Ally Challenge. We're interested in rallying more support for this movement, and engaging more men and organizations to partner with us for gender equality. Countless tales and data in our research point to the importance of an inclusive approach to finally bridge this divide. Men want their wives, daughters, and other women to succeed. Women want to feel supported and included, personally and professionally. We want the same thing. We need each other to make it happen. Men, join us if you have not already. Let men support you if you have not already. We're in this to win together.

---

[10]   Valerio and Sawyer, "The Men Who Mentor Women," https://hbr.org/2016/12/the-men-who-mentor-women.

WE HAVE A SOLID FOUNDATION TO BUILD UPON

What "Good" Looks Like

Sheryl Sandberg, an executive at Facebook and author of *Lean In*[11] and *Option B*,[12] is a great example of what "good" looks like. Her voice continues to push us to lean in and ask for what we want rather than expect someone to ask us. When I read *Lean In* in 2011, my biggest takeaway was: men are really good at asking for what they want. They come ready with facts and show confidence. Women tend to shy away from their achievements, minimizing them, and hoping someone will notice them when it's time for a promotion or pay increase. Again, with stagnant increases for females in leadership, this theme is still relevant today. What Sheryl did, however, was change the conversation from victim-mode to survivor-mode, providing a robust set of solutions rather than problems. She brought awareness – not just to the statistics, but the root causes behind them.

Two years following the loss of her husband, she is providing another set of tools with *Option B*. This book demonstrates the keys to becoming resilient and finding joy in your life. As women, we often do not separate the personal vs. professional spheres of our lives. In the converse, I have never had a group of male leaders ask for a workshop on work-life balance! Sharing her vulnerability as a single mom, teaching her children how to build resilience, finding joy

---

[11]   Sandberg, *Lean In: Women, Work, and the Will to Lead*, 1-387.

[12]   Sandberg, *Option B: Facing Adversity, Building Resilience, and Finding Joy*, 1-240.

in a not-so-perfect world, Sheryl discusses the strong male allies who came alongside her. She's found mentors she could emulate, managers who gave her space to succeed on her own, and sponsors supporting her when she was not in the room.

Although we have not had a woman president in the U.S., we did have an amazing leader in Michelle Obama. Politics aside, Barack Obama set the tone for what "good" looks like for male allyship. He promoted females into leadership positions, championed a woman to replace him, supported his daughters, and empowered his wife to stand beside him as an equal. Michelle, like Hillary, outpaced her husband's successes in law school and early in her career. Yet, she decided to champion his success and stand beside him. This is an incredibly personal choice she made in partnership with her family, doing what she felt was best for all.

Vulnerability guru, Brené Brown, helps us understand what "good" looks like. In her famous TEDTalk and her three bestselling books, she outlines strategies to embrace shame and be authentic based on your own accord.[13] She gives everyone permission to be themselves, to share their stories, and stop apologizing for who they are. As women, we're good at being vulnerable, yet we often lack confidence. Vulnerability without confidence loses impact. In her research, Brené teaches us how to conquer our fears and share our story in an open and inviting way. By opening up ourselves and sharing our fears and limitations, we invite people into our lives to help us – personally and professionally.

What We Know from HIStory

I recall, as you likely do, asking a childhood history teacher, "Why do we have to learn this? It's in the past." The reply: "If we do not learn about our history, we are destined to repeat it." As a middle schooler, this was confusing; today, it has far more application. HIStory, phonetically breaks down to his-story. It exists for us to learn and be stronger moving forward. However, history books largely focus on the male figures. We now know there have been many more

---

[13] "The Power of Vulnerability," last modified March 16, 2012, https://www.ted.com/talks/brene_brown_on_vulnerability.

significant females in history than the books cite. We can learn valuable lessons by looking back on significant women in history.

The women's suffrage movement, in the United States, officially began in 1848 with a group of abolitionist activists – mostly women, with some men – gathering to discuss rights. This group advocated, "We hold these truths to be self-evident that all men and women are created equal, that they are endowed by their Creator with certain inalienable rights. That among these are life, liberty, and the pursuit of happiness."[14] Among other things, this meant they believed we should have the right to vote. Yet, the journey wasn't completed until 1920.

There were many setbacks along the way, including tugs of war between the women leaders, the Civil War, and the priority of civil rights issues, and with competing political views. When the suffragettes shifted the approach, they achieved results. Instead of arguing women deserved the same rights and responsibilities as men because women and men were "created equal," the leaders began arguing women deserved the right to vote because they were different from men. They took advantage of their role as the domestic caretaker and leveraged it as a political virtue. Their so-called, "maternal commonwealth." This tactic proved successful in speaking to the political parties' needs at the time, and signals some lessons learned for women today.

First, male support makes a difference. Engaging men early in the conversation created male allies to carry the message forward to other men. Because male-only gatherings were commonplace at the time, women had to leverage male support to spread the message. Today, most C-suites and leadership teams are over 80% male. We still need men to support the conversation when we are not in the room. Second, awareness-raising is not enough. Early on, the suffragettes garnered the interest of men. However, to garner the mass appeal, they had to shift their strategy to draw more men into the conversation. Today, this means fostering more men supporting women. We need to shift our focus, aligning with men's values and what's in it for men (WIIFM) to get them on board ... as our foremothers did.

---

[14] "Seneca Falls Convention Begins," last modified 2010, http://www.history.com/this-day-in-history/seneca-falls-convention-begins.

The next significant landmark in the women's movement was in 1972 when Title IX passed. It outlined "No person in the United States shall, on the basis of sex, be excluded from participation in, be denied the benefits of, or be subjected to discrimination under any education program or activity receiving federal financial assistance."[15] This paved the way for females in sports and in college advancement. More women than men graduate from college today (39% compared to 32%) according to The Condition of Education 2016 report.[16] Although the pay gap remains, examples of the US women's soccer and hockey teams underscore its importance. It takes time to create positive change.

One of our favorite discoveries during our research was the result of looking for "Title IX" information online. Most of the articles center on the perception of loss for men. Key phrases such as "it was done at the expense of men,"[17] and "colleges cut men's programs to satisfy Title IX,"[18] signal a perception of lose-win. Again, we learn from this history. As women advance, we need to change the perception of men losing for us to win. It is a win-win. The women's movement still has today's male leaders leery because of this perception of lose-win. It's not a zero sum game, as we will outline in section three. We can all make the pie bigger together, rather than cutting it in larger or smaller pieces.

This brings us to 1993. The Family and Medical Leave Act (FMLA) was passed, requiring covered employers to provide eligible employees with job protection and unpaid leave for qualified medical and family reasons. This guarantees eligible employees up to 12 work weeks of unpaid leave each year with no threat of job loss or health care benefits.[19] Although this still does not equal the playing field for working mothers, this legislation accommodates us when we have children or are the caregivers of aging family members. This

15 "Title IX and Sex Discrimination," last modified April 2015. https://www2.ed.gov/about/offices/list/ocr/docs/tix_dis.html.

16 "The Condition of Education 2016," last modified May 26, 2016. https://nces.ed.gov/pubsearch/pubsinfo.asp?pubid=2016144.

17 "Title IX's Dark Legacy," last modified June 22, 2012, https://www.usnews.com/opinion/articles/2012/06/22/title-ixs-dark-legacy.

18 "Colleges Cut Men's Programs to Satisfy Title IX," last modified May 1, 2011, http://www.nytimes.com/2011/05/02/sports/02gender.html?mcubz=2.

19 "Family and Medical Leave Act," last modified July 29, 2017, https://www.dol.gov/whd/fmla/.

granted many women the flexibility to care for their families without the fear of job loss, and we have seen some gains in leadership roles since its passing.

This, as well as our other wins, signal some lessons learned. First, this act was championed largely by President Bill Clinton. It was one of his signature accomplishments, alongside Hillary's focus on health care reform. Partnering together works, yet it was a small step towards gender equality. In fact, the U.S. is the only country among 41 developed nations not mandating any paid leave for new parents, according to data compiled by the Organization for Economic Cooperation and Development. In the National Compensation Survey of 2016, only 13% of U.S. private companies offer workers some kind of paid maternity leave, and very few offer any paternity leave.[20]

With 40% of US families with children relying on the mother as the sole or primary breadwinner (data collected by the Pew Research Center), this is troubling.[21] Many organizations have workarounds requiring women to take disability or short-term medical leave to be compensated partially for their time. I know I was appalled to call having a child a 'disability.' I had some fun with it and changed my out of office to "Out on Disability." My clients were alarmed until they learned I was having a baby. Yet another lesson learned: sometimes we must share our story to be heard as women.

Our foremothers and their male allies paved the way for our success. Today, there are more men speaking up with us in organizations and with our families to propel positive change. We need more of them to close these gaps and achieve equality together.

What We Learn from Men and Women Leaders

Here's a sneak peek of some of the male allies we got to meet along the way in our research for ONE. It showcases stories of men supportive as sponsors, mentors, coaches, advocates, and managers.

---

[20] "TED: The Economics Daily," last modified November 4, 2016, https://www.bls.gov/opub/ted/2016/13-percent-of-private-industry-workers-had-access-to-paid-family-leave-in-march-2016.htm.

[21] "Breadwinner Moms," last modified May 29, 2013, http://www.pewsocialtrends.org/2013/05/29/breadwinner-moms/.

The first is John, a former senior leader for a large pharmaceuticals company. John has had a strong feminine influence in his personal life – his grandmother, mother, and wife – as well as professionally with strong female executives. He recalled vivid examples of championing women throughout his career. One centered on a senior level succession planning meeting. As he describes,

> "There were some questions from the other white males in the room about a high-potential African American woman. There was no female from the senior staff present. All white males. This was 1993, so not uncommon ... and not uncommon still today. Yet, there was a question about this person's capability. I stepped into the conversation and championed her. I stated to the group, 'She's been doing this work at an excellent level for years. I think you guys need to figure out whether you're going to make a move on her or not because she's certainly not going to be around here for a long period of time if you guys don't figure out where you're going with this high potential employee.'
>
> I went to bat for her in the meeting. I then followed up with her supervisor and made my case. Six months later she received a significant promotion. Now, I can't say this was entirely due to me. Obviously, her performance was the key factor, but there's a moment in time when somebody has to just say, 'put up or shut up.'"

This is what male allies do: they speak up for us when we are not in the room. They leverage their voice, and are vulnerable as they challenge the norm.

The second sneak peek is Jen. Jen is a senior sales leader at the largest global animal health organization. When we spoke with her, she had two kids under age five and a husband who worked full-time. She was recently promoted, and as she looked at her peers, she was the only person without a stay-at-home spouse. She candidly shared this observation in the internal interview process, and drew the boundaries for work-life plan. Her story is one of success because she was self-aware and asked for what she wanted. Jen shared in our interview that she has had many men supporting her along the way. One of her managers, early in her career, pulled her aside after a meeting she facilitated.

"That was phenomenal. You just blew me away. You should have seen the room. You had their attention." She had no idea, no knowledge of her ability. He proactively gave her opportunities based on the abilities he saw. This built her confidence. This same manager, at a national conference, asked the team members to introduce themselves to senior leadership. She remembered thinking, "What do I have to say that's worthwhile?" Confidently, she said the right thing…and learned networking is paramount for career success.

As managers, men have a vital role in promoting women and building their confidence. Recognizing achievements and providing opportunities for them to build relationships and access to leadership is key.

Research confirms having male mentors is key. Even the word mentor phonetically implies a male role, men-tor. Men are socialized to give advice and solve problems for others. We often think our mentors should be female, but this approach has less chance of being successful. For one thing, there are not many women at the top to choose from! In our interviews with female leaders, many shared having men as mentors – showing them what "good" looks like – was a clear differentiator.

They cited these men helped them talk through difficult situations or navigate their career path, and some provided candid feedback when they needed to hear it. I still remember having a male mentor tell me I said "like" and "um" a lot and I needed to work on my audible pauses. He said it took away from my message and made me sound less intelligent than he knew me to be. My first dose of radical candor, and I benefited from the intentional feedback. It got my attention. Men mentor women because they care and tell them what they *need* to hear (not necessarily what they *want* to hear). Strong male mentors provide an example for us to follow.

HOW TO NAVIGATE THIS BOOK

To change these stagnant statistics and to be the highest performing organization possible, we need women and men at the top leading together. This means working collaboratively side-by-side, as true allies, to get this done. Our title – ONE – is a symbol of this inclusion, everyone together, united on challenges for both genders. ONE means we choose to view each other as human vs. by stereotypes, we focus on support vs. competition, we believe in potential vs. bias, and we embrace positive change together.

Based on our research, we found a set of techniques, tools, and strategies for us all to implement together –

- Heart
- Story
- Speak
- Work-Life

Each aligns to a section of this book, giving you simple-to-follow steps. Each section has content for both male allies and women leaders. Action steps, for building your plans, are available as appropriate.

We recommend reading both points of view. While the perspectives are different, the strategies mirror one another. When all leaders employ these strategies together, they work in lock step, facilitating success. When we use a common approach and common language, we become ONE.

We encourage men and women to utilize these proven strategies:

- Heart: "Channeling the Women You Empathize" for male allies, and "Starting the Dialogue with the WIIFM" (what's in it for men) for women leaders
- Story: "Asking for HERStory" for male allies, and "Sharing Your Story" for women leaders
- Speak: "Speaking up with Her" for male allies, and "Speaking Up with Him" for women leaders
- Work-Life: "Doing the Fair Share at Home" for male allies, and "Practicing Self-Care" for women leaders

Enjoy the stories canvassing different roles, cultures, organizations, industries, genders, and generations. Our goal is having you walk away with tangible and practical ideas on how to get more involved in the movement. Dive into your section of choice; there is no need to read sequentially. Think of this as a menu of strategies – pick one that works for you and learn how to apply it in your journey for gender equality. Get involved personally and you will raise awareness and spread positive momentum to the movement overall. It is only through working together across genders that all human beings achieve equality.

SECTION TWO: HEART

MALE ALLIES CHANNEL THE WOMEN THEY EMPATHIZE

Think About What You Want for Your Daughter, Mother, or Spouse

Many of our male allies had a common tie: strong women in their lives. Whether this was their mother, aunt, or grandmother growing up, or their daughters or wives, they had seen the power and benefits of having these relationships. We began our research with a curiosity for where this desire originated. The answer was simple: men channel the women they empathize, giving them a source of inspiration to support other females. While women in our research do not want to be treated as daughters or mother figures, they respond to empathy from a genuine place.

This is best illustrated through Eric's story.

"I support gender equality because I don't know anything different. When I was growing up, my parents divorced when I was in second grade, so I grew up with my mother and my sister. I'm used to having majority women in the house. They are always going to be equal, but different. I clearly recognize the differences between men and women, obviously physically, and sometimes how we behave. I recognize my daughters have different personalities, and I support them in whatever it is they want to do. Supporting them and their ambitions, but recognizing we have differences in the way each of them approach problems, and they are different than the way I approach problems.

For men, I think the biggest thing is if you are fortunate enough to have daughters, find something unique to bond with them. For me it's our monthly daddy-daughter doughnut day. We have open conversations as a father and daughter, because that relationship is going to set the example for how she interacts with men personally and professionally. Have those conversations with her. It's not only about dating. A father should have conversations with his daughter about work-life.

A father should have conversations with his daughter about her career aspirations. It's okay to play dress up and play dolls, hair, makeup, whatever it is, but it's good to have conversations with your daughter about, 'What do you want to do long-term? What makes you want to do those things? What challenges do you see? How can I help you overcome those challenges?' I'm a big advocate of fathers being heavily involved in their daughters' lives."

While this is not necessary to being a male ally, each interviewee had a strong calling based on his relationships with women in the formative years. For them, the fight is personal. They do not see females as different. Male allies see them as people, as human beings. While there are clear biological differences, the passion for helping them comes from a human connection, regardless of them being a woman or a man. They want to be a part of the conversation because they want to help. It comes from a genuine positive place. While early male allies tend to lack the known unconscious biases towards gender, this is not as natural for men overall. We found, in our research, these traits can be learned as well. We hope the stories from these men, and strategies provided here, will lay the foundation for you to build your plan.

Jim, a vocal male ally managing partner in a financial services firm shared,

"I grew up non-traditionally and my mother was a single mom. She put herself through nursing school and she took care of me without even skipping a beat. When you can look back and say, I didn't really realize we had issues because mom was taking care of things, I think that speaks volumes to her capabilities, her strengths, and her wisdom. Not only was she the caregiver, but the financial giver, the direction giver, and the advice giver. She was all of those things to me. I learned from her example and want to be there for other women as a support mechanism. I learned from her that all people are different. I want to be able to foster that same kind of encouragement for other women in my life."

Jim has transferred this strong tie from his mother to clients he works for and advocates for in his community. He sings his wife's praises for the work she does to maintain the family and her career, and is a highly involved father. He proudly shares women's successes on social media and his firm sponsors their professional development events regularly as a dedication to the cause. His story reveals a deeper understanding of where this passion originated: his mother, a pioneer in women's advancement.

As a spouse, men have an important male ally role to play as well. Regional Business Director of a large animal health company, Kristin says,

"I got feedback from my male mentor that I was ready to make a career change, and it was up to me to network with key leaders making those decisions. He said I needed to make sure leadership understood who I was and what I was about. Six months later, I had an opportunity requiring a move to New Jersey. Thankfully, my spouse, who is amazing, supported me and decided, 'Yes, I will uproot my career, too. We will go to New Jersey.' Because of his support, I grew the most in the shortest amount of time in my career. It was the most transformational part of my career because it took me out of my comfort, confident zone and put me – overnight – into being stretched."

Kristin's story emphasizes the dual roles (personal and professional) male allies play in setting their mentees or partners up for success. Because of her mentor's guidance in seeing change before it happened and her husband's unwavering support to prioritize her career move, she had a recipe for success.

For men seeking to be more of a male ally, think deeply about the women in your life you care about. Chances are, several have had a positive impact on you. Often, by paying it forward, you feel the benefits of giving far greater than the receiver does. It feels good to help others, especially those with the greatest needs.

This adage surfaced frequently in our research: "It's fun to root for the underdog."

Look for a Woman You Can Positively Impact

As we have outlined, today's senior leadership teams continue to be largely comprised of men. Men featured in our interviews often served the role as a confidant, someone a woman could candidly speak with and trust. Primarily as managers, male allies can lift those around them by recognizing their accomplishments, giving them credit for their ideas publically, challenging them with new opportunities, or through simple day-to-day support. Kim's story illustrates a beautiful example of the subtle ways men support women.

Kim, a CEO at a successful women's leadership foundation, was interviewing for her first president position.

> "I told the male hiring manager, 'You have to trust me that I know where I need to be. I have different parts of my life. My family is number one. I go to church every Friday morning. My kids go to Catholic school. Trust I know where I need to be given my responsibilities. If that's not going to work for you, then this is not right.' He looked at me and said, 'You know what? I've been married four times. I have five children from three wives ranging from two to twenty one. You have your priorities right.'"

This male ally became an incredible source of support for Kim, helping remove obstacles for her, getting out of her way and letting her do her job. Most importantly, he trusted her to do it correctly. The business doubled its results when she was president, and Kim has had several president and CEO roles subsequently. It all started with this male ally taking a chance on – and trusting – her.

He may or may not have been looking for a woman to diversify his team. He wanted the right person for the right role, and Kim was it. He was in the perfect position, as her manager and the most senior leader of the organization, for support. Kim's personal story resonated with him due to *his* story. Whatever the connection, "fit" is key. The trust Kim received put her in a position to be successful. She knew he had her back, and she gave it all of her energy (especially when it came to her schedule).

Meet Nate. Nate is author of the book *Raising Supaman*, owns his financial services business, and has always thought of himself as a male ally.[22] Having a strong mother and sister growing up, he said,

> "My closest friends, allies, and closest supporters have primarily been women, so I just feel responsible for giving back to those who have given the most to me. My wife's career trajectory is so much better than mine, but when I met her, I think she was largely under fulfilling her potential. Since then, she's earned a master's degree. She was the first African American principal of our local preparatory school, which is a big deal. She's in the final stages of completing her PhD, has partnered with a number of organizations, and started a consulting enterprise.
>
> There were times we had to decide who was going to 'take the backseat,' because there could only be one up front. When you're a parent with a small child, somebody has to be home, or at least someone should be. I didn't worry about advancing my career. I turned down opportunities to make more money and do other things. I wanted to make sure my wife and son both had a chance to fulfill their potential. And, now to see our son grown up, successful, it's all worked out for our family."

Nate's story demonstrates how, through support of his wife's success and career, his family benefited. He's found his passion along the way for parenting through being a huge part of his son's life. His work at the Raising Supaman Project leverages his and his family's experiences with parenting and education,

---

22 Tuner, *Raising Supaman*, 1

and how to raise the best possible children. His recognition of his wife's potential and making his career choices based objectively on potential rather than traditional gender roles is a perfect example of what a good male ally looks like. It does not mean sacrificing your career; it means making decisions based on what is best for your family and each partner's potential.

To men who want to be involved, we say: women everywhere can benefit from your support! From our expert interviews, we found the most common ways men support females personally and professionally are:

- Being their voice when they are not there.
- Speaking up with them when they are not heard.
- Asking them questions to learn more about them and what they want.
- Listening to their ideas.
- Giving them feedback to recognize success and develop new skills.
- Challenging them with new opportunities.
- Connecting them with those who can best lend support.
- Seeing their potential rather than seeking proof of accomplishments.
- Trusting them to craft a path to success.
- Balancing work/life management challenges.

When we assembled these top ten support mechanisms, we were astounded by the common denominator – communication.

As you rifle through your brain's contact list of women who could value these support mechanisms, prioritize those who can benefit from your strengths. Where will you likely have the biggest impact? By prioritizing the need and your ability to meet it, you create the best position to succeed together. It really is a simple supply and demand equation.

Be Her Ally, Not Her Father

With women in mind who can benefit from two simple criteria – impact pared with strengths – it is important to hit home on another theme from our research. They do not want father figures at work – the knight in shining armor, the man who takes them under his wing, the patriarch doting on them, publically. This is opposite of a male ally. A male ally gets out of their way and lets them succeed on their own merits. From a young age, men are socialized to save the day for women. Countless fairy tales reinforce this message. Yet, they can save themselves. They need support from male allies to increase the chances of success. They can do it alone, but it is important to note research shows it takes a significantly longer time to achieve results by themselves. The Centered Leadership Project studies female leaders. Its book, *How Remarkable Women Lead*, notes, "While we've met women leaders who have succeeded without a sponsor, there is no doubt having a sponsor on your team is a huge advantage. It's not a one-way street. The giver gains fulfillment from his acts of kindness and giving."[23]

This groundbreaking book on leadership chronicles successful women with proven strategies for success. It aligns with our research on the importance of sponsorship (which is different from mentorship). Authors Joanna Barsh and Susie Cranston explain, "There is a difference between sponsors and mentors. Mentors dispense wisdom whereas sponsors get involved. A sponsor believes in you, and a mentor may not go that far."[24] Our male allies described their involvement as dispensing transactional advice. They stepped up and spoke up, asked, and challenged as needed. Mentors, an important role for men not to be overlooked, is not as powerful as sponsorship. It is important to think of the role you will play – mentor or sponsor. Both are keys to her success.

To be a true male ally, you must be vulnerable. This word is often thought to mean "femininity," which isn't appealing to men. The gender tightrope is real. As one male ally defined, "Vulnerability is the "self-esteem to do what's right." Vulnerability is pivotal, and is why male allies are remarkable and selfless. They put the others around them before themselves, and root for the underdog. In our interviews, men continually downplayed their efforts, giving all the credit to the women. Common themes emerged – "She did all the work," or "She had it in her all along." They do not take credit for what she accomplished with their nudges and support. Many commented, "Why wouldn't I support them? It's the right thing to do." This vulnerability and selflessness on the part of the male ally is critical.

---

[23]   Barsh and Cranston, *How Remarkable Women Lead*, 173.

[24]   Ibid, 131.

Elaine, a business owner and government leader, shared that her father and husband have been huge supporters, always "having her back." When she entered the workforce, she welcomed male allies' support.

> "In one of the first jobs I had with the bank, there was an individual who recruited me to move into a different division, and he was very much a supporter. He felt like, 'You can do this. We're choosing you to do this. We want you.' He, for many years, then was someone who always said, 'Keep moving forward,' and helped me rise in my career."

Not only did this male ally encourage Elaine, he helped open doors for her to new opportunities where he saw her potential leading ... not waiting until she proved herself to earn the opportunity.

Studies confirm men are often assessed based on potential and women are often assessed on performance, often having to prove it again to earn respect.[25] Yet, if we never have someone take a risk on us, we will never have the opportunity to provide results. We need male allies to take a chance based on belief rather than facts or a perfect track record. This requires real vulnerability, trusting she can do it without having past results to prove it.

Many women in our research commented their male allies "saw something in me I did not see in myself," similar to Elaine's story. They are visionaries who see beyond the person in front of them today; they see what's possible for her in the future. It's not surprising many of these men had strong females while growing up. This translated to a belief system where women leaders are welcomed. And, if they did not have the privilege when younger, their daughters, female leaders around them, and their wives inspire them today. They see what they will become, not merely what they are today.

One caution for men channeling these feelings and empathy: women in our research tended to feel frustrated when men shared their purpose as "Because I have a daughter or mother." It does not mean you know what it is like to be a

---

[25] Barnett and Rivers, *How The "New Discrimination" Is Holding Women Back*, http://www.catalyst.org/zing/how-new-discrimination-holding-women-back.

woman. When sharing your "why" for being a male ally, focus on what you see in her *specifically* that motivates you to support her. We found in our research men often get even more from the relationship than the women. It feels good to give.

Gender equality and mentoring experts, and authors of *Athena Rising: How and Why Men Should Mentor Women*, Brad Johnson and David Smith, shared with us,

> "For men looking to be more of a male ally, think about the business case, and how organizations benefit from more women leaders. Then, think about what is good for her, channeling the women you know and how your mentorship could benefit them most. Guys benefit from broader networks, too, and are seen as talent developers in organizations when they support women. Often, we find organizations reward male allies with more career opportunities longer-term. It also improves men's emotional intelligence as they surround themselves with people who may think differently than they do."[26]

As Brad and David outline, men who are "all in" often benefit more than the women. It starts with one key decision to channel the person, then decide who you will support, and how. It is important you support genuinely, leveraging your strengths.

Male Ally Action Steps

For male allies looking to channel the empathy for women leaders and gender equality, here are the action steps to reflect on to being an even stronger male ally. In sections ahead you will find action steps to guide your journey.

1. List all of the important women – past and currently – from your personal and professional life. Write down why they inspire you.

---

[26] Johnson and Smith, *Athena Rising: How and Why Men Should Mentor Women*, 1-224.

2. Make another list of the women you care about personally and/ or professionally *today*. Prioritize the list based on your ability to positively impact them with your strengths as a mentor, advisor, coach, sponsor, or advocate.

3. Brainstorm strategies to start a dialogue with the women in item #2. Use the bullet points on page 26 for reference.

WOMEN LEADERS START THE DIALOGUE WITH THE WIIFM

WIIFM: What's In It for Men?

Gender diversity drives business performance. This is something both genders benefit from equally. When opportunities, pay, and promotions are based on performance instead of gender biases, organizations thrive. This is a competitive advantage for organizations that get it. When there is gender equality in organizations, teams perform at a higher level and profits are higher.[27] While the male allies we talked to genuinely care about women and offer their support naturally, we all can get behind proven statistics to support a partnership to make this happen.

McKinsey's annual <u>Women Matter</u> report attributes a 16% higher profitability rate with gender equality and states $12 trillion could be added to the U.S. economy by 2025 if companies advance gender equality.[28] They found,

> "...companies in the top quartile for gender or racial and ethnic diversity are more likely to have financial returns above their national industry medians. Companies in the

---

[27] "Women Matter 2016," last modified September 27, 2016, http://www.mckinsey.com/business-functions/organization/our-insights/women-in-the-workplace-2016.

[28] Ibid.

bottom quartile in these dimensions are statistically less likely to achieve above-average returns. And diversity is probably a competitive differentiator that shifts market share toward more diverse companies over time.

While correlation does not equal causation (greater gender and ethnic diversity in corporate leadership doesn't automatically translate into more profit), the correlation does indicate that when companies commit themselves to diverse leadership, they are more successful. More diverse companies, we believe, are better able to win top talent and improve their customer orientation, employee satisfaction, and decision making, and all that leads to a virtuous cycle of increasing returns."

Gender equality practices at organizations signal a sustainable competitive advantage, far more impactful than merely new products or services, better customer service, or strategies that are easy for competitors to copy. By attracting and retaining top talent through proven inclusivity, these organizations thrive long-term. Think about the last time you were on a diverse team, chances are the ideas were more innovative, the team considered more points of view, and the team was more efficient and productive. These behaviors boost performance, and are hard for competitors to match.

An article published by Forbes in 2016, "Male Allies in the Workplace: The First Step is Admitting There's a Problem," cited a research study of 300 male allies who indicated very low awareness of the gender inequities facing women in the workplace.[29] They recommend first making men aware there is a problem. They not only need to be aware of the leadership and pay gaps, but why it is a problem. What gets their attention? Organizations are leaving money on the table … on average, 16% less profitability.

A recent poll from the Pew Research Center builds off this, showing 91% of Americans choosing "agree" to the statement: "It is very important women

[29]   "Male Allies in the Workplace: The First Step Is Admitting There's A Problem," last modified October 6, 2016, https://www.forbes.com/sites/georgenehuang/2016/10/02/male-allies-in-the-workplace-the-first-step-is-admitting-theres-a-problem/#23a90680b721.

have the same rights as men in our country."[30] This is a clear indication they align on beliefs, but not in actions. This is essentially the definition of feminism, yet the men we talked to did not want to be labelled as feminists. They see their beliefs and actions as "normal" for all people. While this is true, we found these men to be more of a rare breed in practice than in belief. Often, when I say, "Male allies see *all* men as allies to women," I get a raised eyebrow followed by the scoff, "They should talk to (insert non-male ally here); not every man is like that."

Let's talk with these men the way they prefer. Rather than ask them to be a full on feminist, let's instead share some facts and engage them in a dialogue. For women looking to engage men in the conversation and gain their support, we recommend the following blueprint. Think of these as talking points to have in your back pocket as you prepare:

- I know you are busy, and I wanted to talk with you about my career path and gender equality at our organization. I see you as a great male ally for women because you have done X, said Y, or believe Z.

- As a woman, I realize there can be unconscious biases impacting our career paths and the pay decisions made at organizations. Gender equality is important to me because when both genders partner together and have inclusive conversations like this, research shows businesses profits are 16% higher.

- Currently, women continue to be paid 83% of what men in similar positions are paid, and only account for 5% of CEOs and 80% of board positions. I have noticed our organization has A% women in leadership and/or B% pay gap. What do you think?

- Supporting gender equality is important to positively drive business performance. We can do this better together than separately. Research supports men as mentors, sponsors, managers, coaches, advocates, and advisors have a big impact on women's success. How do you think you can help women?

Using these facts and questions as a guide, we emphasize: this is a dialogue. Men in our research strongly agreed women have a tendency to

---

[30] "The Narrowing, but Persistent, Gender Pap in Pay," last modified April 3, 2016, http://www.pewresearch.org/fact-tank/2017/04/03/gender-pay-gap-facts/.

dance around difficult conversations, wanting to please their audiences. This fault, in our gender norming, can annoy men. Instead, be direct. Start with the facts and quickly transition into questions involving him in the discussion. Get him talking, get his opinions, get his ideas. The more inclusive we are with men, the more inclusive they will be with us. Remember, men still hold the overwhelming majority of decision-making roles. Leaving them out of important conversations is a mistake. We need their buy-in if we all want to succeed together.

It's Not a Zero Sum Game

We found men resist male allyship primarily due to this fear: "If she gets promoted or is paid as much as I am, I lose something." This math does not compute. Just because there are more women at the table, does not mean there must be fewer men. When profits and business results improve due to more inclusive decision making and leadership, there are more seats at the table. The pie gets bigger for everyone.

As we have highlighted from proven sources such as Catalyst, McKinsey, and the Pew Research Center, the data are there. If you are lucky enough to work at an organization where it is available, educate people and advocate for positive change. Be inclusive with your message, and you are likely to draw men into the conversation along with others. When we asked for the data, most did not know their organization's statistics, yet many commented it is improving, or cited a recent promotion by a strong woman to validate the company and why they worked there. We encourage you to ask your firm for the number of females in leadership roles – the difference in manager representation to senior leader representation is telling – and for numbers on pay by gender. Chances are someone tracks it; they do not share it for fear of backlash. Everyone wants to believe the gender inequity problem is not happening where they are. It is a reality. The numbers do not add up if you think you are an exception.

Michael, gender equality activist and expert, shared this very topic in his recent TEDTalk explaining how this is good for men.[31] He highlighted male privilege and how it is often invisible to men. This has implications for our

---

[31] "Why Gender Equality is Good for Everyone, Men Included," last modified September 16, 2015, https://www.ted.com/talks/michael_kimmel_why_gender_equality_is_good_for_everyone_men_included.

perceptions, where men do not see the obstacles for others who are different. They see those people as less privileged.

While men see us all as humans, women see differences. Women recall differences in treatment based on unconscious biases that are more prevalent for women and minorities. It is hard for men to understand because they have not experienced it. They don't know what they don't know. We need to educate them.

Michael cites a specific example with his story.

> "Recently, at my university where I teach, a colleague and I both teach the Sociology of Gender course on alternate semesters. She gives a guest lecture for me when I teach. I give a guest lecture for her when she teaches. So, I walk into her class to give a guest lecture, about 300 students in the room, and as I walk in, one of the students looks up and says, 'Oh, finally, an objective opinion.'

> Making gender visible to men is the first step to engaging men to support gender equality. Now, when men first hear about gender equality, when they first start thinking about it, they often think, many men think, well, that's right, that's fair, that's just, that's the ethical imperative. But not all men. Some men think – the lightning bolt goes off, and they go, 'Oh my God, yes, gender equality,' and they will immediately begin to mansplain to you your oppression. They see supporting gender equality something akin to the cavalry, like, 'Thanks very much for bringing this to our attention, ladies, we'll take it from here.' This results in a syndrome I like to call 'premature self-congratulation.' There's another group, though, that actively resists gender equality, that sees gender equality as something detrimental to men. I was on a TV talk show opposite four white men. This is the beginning of the book I wrote, 'Angry White Men.'

> These were four angry white men who believed that they, white men in America, were the victims of reverse discrimination in the workplace. And they all told stories about how they were qualified for jobs, qualified for

promotions, they didn't get them, they were really angry. And the reason I'm telling you this is I want you to hear the title of this particular show. It was a quote from one of the men, and the quote was, "A Black Woman Stole My Job." And they all told their stories, qualified for jobs, qualified for promotions, didn't get it, really angry.

And then it was my turn to speak, and I said, 'I have just one question for you guys, and it's about the title of the show, 'A Black Woman Stole My Job.' Actually, it's about one word in the title. I want to know about the word 'my.' Where did you get the idea it was your job? Why isn't the title of the show, 'A Black Woman Got the Job?' or 'A Black Woman Got A Job?' Because without confronting men's sense of entitlement, I don't think we'll ever understand why so many men resist gender equality."

Michael draws more comparisons to consider about overall happiness.

"Gender equality is good for countries. It turns out, according to most studies, those countries that are the most gender equal are also the countries that score highest on the happiness scale. And that's not just because they're in Europe. It is also good for companies. Research by Catalyst and others has shown conclusively that the more gender-equal companies are, the better it is for workers, the happier their labor force is. They have lower job turnover.

They have lower levels of attrition. They have an easier time recruiting. They have higher rates of retention, higher job satisfaction, higher rates of productivity. So the question I'm often asked in companies is, 'Boy, this gender equality thing, that's really going to be expensive, huh?' And I say, 'Oh no, in fact, what you have to start calculating is how much gender inequality is already costing you. It is extremely expensive.' So it is good for business.

It's good for men. It is good for the kind of lives we want to live, because young men especially have changed enormously, and they want to have lives that are animated by terrific relationships with their children. They expect their partners, their spouses, their wives, to work outside the home and be as committed to their careers as they are. Now, it turns out the more egalitarian our relationships, the happier both partners are. Data from psychologists and sociologists are quite persuasive here. I think we have the persuasive numbers, to prove to men gender equality is not a zero-sum game, but a win-win.

Here's what the data show. When men begin the process of engaging with balancing work and family, we often have two phrases we use to describe what we do. We pitch in and we help out. Because here's what the data show: when men share housework and childcare, their children do better in school. Their children have lower rates of absenteeism, higher rates of achievement. They are less likely to be diagnosed with ADHD. They are less likely to see a child psychiatrist. They are less likely to be put on medication."

A theme we will delve into in section five, practicing self-care, is key as well. Michael continues,

"When men share housework and childcare, their wives are happier. Duh. Not only that, their wives are healthier. Their wives are less likely to see a therapist, less likely to be diagnosed with depression, less likely to be put on medication, more likely to go to the gym, report higher levels of marital satisfaction. So when men share housework and childcare, their wives are happier and healthier, and men certainly want this as well.

When men share housework and childcare, the men are healthier. They smoke less, drink less, and take recreational drugs less often. They are less likely to go to the ER but more likely to go to a doctor for routine screenings. They are less likely to see a therapist, less likely to be diagnosed with depression, less likely to be taking prescription medication. So when men share housework and childcare, the men are happier and healthier. And who wouldn't want that? And finally, when men share housework and childcare, they have more sex."

Elaine reinforces this message from her perspective. As a senior executive for a state organization creating jobs, she shares,

"Women becoming more active in the workforce, coming up to equality, benefits men in so many ways. It benefits women, too. I would have said, 'I'd gladly exchange roles. I'd love that idea of running the household and taking care of the kids and doing all those kinds of things. That suits me well.' Then men have the option. Once they see that if they support women in their roles, that option's open to them, maybe they'd be more active in trying to be supporters of equality. We're in this together, and we must show the benefits everyone can have and the flexibility everyone can have if women can be a more equal participants in all aspects of our life, from working, to home life, to community life. We win together."

Elaine and Michael tie a nice box around all the facts supporting men being involved in the conversation. They have happier lives, their businesses perform better, and they have better relationships with the families. When we spoke with Michael, he affirmed our strategies: engaging men in the dialogue, sharing your story, asking for it, and practicing self-care. He's an expert on gender equality and an early advocate for male allyship. We need more Michaels to succeed, and women need to initiate the dialogue to get male allies involved.

Chris, a leader in the financial services industry and vocal male ally, was featured in a blog as a male ally to an incredible industry leader, JT. Chris suspects what motivated to be a male ally will encourage more men on the fringe. He explains,

"One, it expands your network significantly. Two, you feel good about it when you can connect with people outside of your way of thinking. Three, you start to bring the organization or your efforts further along because you have these partners feeling included.

Then, certainly, four is: I would say if you're a parent and you have young daughters, you've heard these old adages a father is a daughter's first love. A daughter often looks for the same kind of traits in a partner in life as those her father demonstrates. Those are two really big things hanging over my head, and I feel great about it living up to them, but I think about them very often. Although my girls are young teenagers right now, every decision I make in front of them, I channel my 26-year-old daughter and think about her reaction. How would she view this?"

Chris' take reinforces themes of men channeling women they care about, and for better networking, thinking, and performance. His firm continues to attract and retain more females than the industry average – leading to better business performance – as a result of its inclusive approach.

What man would not want to be a male ally when he knows all he stands to gain?

Give Men the Chance to Give

Men are wired to respond to data and facts. When you start the dialogue with the WIIFM, pack your discussion with facts and stories, peppered with questions. This is where we see women cop out, feeling selfish for allowing others to help us. To avoid this, we recommend you practice conversations with men who are potential male allies to learn more and feel more comfortable with an uncomfortable conversation.

You must start these conversations from a positive place expressing upbeat intent and passion. Start with the WIIFM. We traditionally use this framework in our leadership coaching – WIIFM – "What's in it for me?" (although in this book, the 'M' stands for 'Men'). This is exactly where people start thinking, even with the most positive changes. We begin with how it impacts us individually. Even the most selfless people are wired to think in survival mode: fight or flight, what does the change mean for me?

And, our primal brains overly focus on loss over gain. This is called loss aversion. Our qualitative research indicates a strong connection between male allies and women they care about personally and professionally. These connections, whether daughters, mothers, peers, or mentors, have a multiplier effect in their sphere of influence. Help them overcome the natural loss aversion and look at the change positively.

Throughout our research, women admitted to struggling with others helping them. Yet, for us to help others, we must first help ourselves. It's important to remember others – including men – want to give to us; give them the chance. It's not weakness, it is a sign of strength to open up, share your story, and accept mentorship, sponsorship, advice, advocacy, or connection … whatever he is best suited to provide. Pair up with men best aligning with your needs.

McKinsey's <u>Women Matter</u> reports key findings cite, "…of the 2,200 employees we surveyed, more than 88% said they do not believe their company is doing what it takes to improve gender diversity, and 62% do not know how to contribute to gender diversity. Shockingly, only 7% have diversity of any kind as a top three priority on their strategic plan,"[32] choosing more tactical priorities focusing on short-term gains rather than the longer-term benefits of diversity.

The report continues, "Regarding the effectiveness of gender-diversity programs, only 40% of respondents reported that these were well implemented in their companies." We find this to be true consistently in our work with females in leadership. Many women's groups we work with have no budget, limited access to supporting resources, and often ineffectively gather to talk about "women's issues" without the presence of men (the majority of decision makers).

If we expect to create positive change, how will we ever do it without the involvement of men? Let male allies support you.

Most men want to help; they just don't know how. Break the ice and start the dialogue. Positive change begins with you.

---

[32] "Women Matter 2016," last modified September 27, 2016, http://www.mckinsey.com/business-functions/organization/our-insights/women-in-the-workplace-2016.

Women Leader Action Steps

Here are some steps to build a plan to enlist the support of men in your careers or at your organizations. You'll find additional steps in the sections on sharing your story, speaking up with him, and practicing self-care.

1. What are your talking points to support the WIIFM and questions you will ask the men? Reference page 33 for some pointers.

2. Ask your organization for the number of women in leadership roles, manager and senior leadership, and for numbers on pay by gender. Share win-win strategies and advocate for positive change.

3. How will you give male allies the chance to give to you?

SECTION THREE:
STORY

WOMEN LEADERS SHARE THEIR STORIES

Know Your "Why"

Women who know what they want are women who win. Often, we struggle to share our story, assuming others around us already know, or will ask if they want to learn more. This is a common mistake – people do not know what we know. We assume our thoughts or beliefs are somehow magically transmitted to those who can support us. Not true. We wait for someone to tap us on the shoulder and ask us what we want. Instead, proactive communication is key. When we proactively communicate our strengths and passions, we are far more likely to achieve success.

Shauna, an African-American District Sales Manager, reflected,

> "I was raised to keep my head down and do good work. And good things come from good work. What I've learned throughout my career is that I need to have a better sense of myself and reality in order to be successful. For me to be successful, I needed to recognize my differences and understand how to leverage them, and I also needed to create deep relationships with people that help me understand how to progress my career – men and women."

Shauna's story hits a key theme in our research. We often assume our good work will be recognized and don't take credit for our ideas. Those opportunities will magically find us ... right? Men speak up, share what they want, and advocate for their careers. Women need to self-promote more, which requires us to know our "why." Rather than assume our colleagues are aware of what makes us tick and what we are passionate about, we need to proactively share our stories.

If you are at a pivot point and not sure of your "why," reflect on the tasks/goals which:

- Get you most excited.
- You do/reach on your very best days.
- When accomplished, continuously garner praise from others.
- You accomplish most efficiently.

We call these the skills and wills. The combination often yields our unique purposes. If you are at a career crossroads, try our self-guided exercise. We encourage you to brainstorm as many words or phrases as possible. Ask your friends, family, peers, managers, sponsors, and male allies for input. They will make your list better. Then, circle the themes that emerge. We often find the intersection of the skills and wills bring to life a unique purpose you can align your work to. This is an area where the support of our male allies is a game changer. Rather than ask those like you, ask those who are different from you. Chances are your male allies will see things you do not see in yourself.

John is a male ally for Shauna. She describes her take on his support.

> "John was one of the first supporters who really advocated for my career. Prior to John, I only had one other manager that gave me consistent and direct coaching. Every time I would ask my managers for feedback, they would say, 'Oh yeah, you did great, it was great, that relationship you have with this person is great.' They didn't really give me a lot of feedback to help me get better. Then, I started working with John. I thrived working with him because he saw something in me and thought I was capable of doing more than I think even I knew I could.
>
> And he was really determined to work with me to make those things happen. He constantly was delivering great

feedback to me and he knew my stress lines. So when I was stressed, or not being myself, he would say, 'Hey, you're exhibiting some of those stress behaviors.' Which at the time was kind of funny to me. I hadn't had someone put the mirror up to me that way. And on the other end, he was very open to giving me autonomy and letting me take risks and try things my way. John was the first person who gave me enough rope to hang myself but he didn't believe I would. And that's really the truth of my relationship with him. I knew I had an ally in him.

John connected me with other people and he told my story behind the scenes to build my brand in relationships. And he helped instill confidence in me that helped me create more allies, male and female, based on the confidence I had and he mirrored that really well for me. He showed me how to do it, which was huge."

John is also a male ally of mine. I find Shauna's take similar to my experience in working with him. John sees something we often do not see in ourselves. He acts as a mirror, coaching women to success. When you know your "why," can collaborate with a strong male ally, and leverage his relationships, you are far more likely to reach the next level. Male allies shared with me a fear: their direct feedback may make women emotional. This sometimes makes the men shy away from sharing …fear of the tears. Yes, we do have biological differences and there are data showing a higher frequency in tears with women than men on average.[33] However, tears can often be a positive thing. Do not hide your emotions, manage them. When your male ally knows your "why" and coaches you with feedback, let him. Remind yourself he is coming from a good place and is helping you become better.

Zeroing in on our "why" lays the foundation for feedback and coaching. When Shauna knew what she wanted, she leveraged John's coaching and feedback. Through his "mirror," she saw a path forward she may not have found on her own. Let men help us see what we may not see for ourselves.

---

[33] Johnson and Smith, Athena Rising: How and Why Men Should Mentor Women, 1-224.

Have a Plan

Women with a plan have an 80% higher chance of success,[34] and it is critical to base it on our "why." Your purpose is the foundation to any successful plan or strategy. It's pivotal to set goals and time chunk action steps to get there. When we channel our "why" into our short- and long-term objectives, it begins to feel more achievable and attainable. The great thing about keeping your plan simple is you can easily communicate it to your male allies. You can align your plan with the organization's aims, creating a win-win for both you and your organization.

Jen, successful CEO and founder of multiple technology companies, shared her approach to career planning with her team.

> "At my organization, we have a career development plan that really levels the playing field for women and men. Every year, we commit to sitting down with all of our employees, one-on-one, to assess where they are and where they want to be. We ask questions. 'What do you do well?' 'What do you want to learn?' 'What do you want to do in three years' (whether with us, or with another company)? 'What are the things you need to do to make it happen?' It is a commitment, and we have not lost an employee in the last three years. In fact, this tool helps retain our top talent.
>
> We have had times when we sat down with someone who was not performing, and asked these questions. It improved their chances of success. Sometimes, we place someone in a different role. Most often, employees own their plan and improve their performance as a result. Women sometimes hold back asking for what they want; this is a way to encourage them to speak up and set the expectation. We want to know what they want."

Jen's story illustrates two key best practices for organizations wanting to close gaps with women in leadership. First, have a process for equally

---

[34] "Study Focuses on Strategies for Achieving Goals," last modified August 26, 2011, http://www.dominican.edu/dominicannews/study-highlights-strategies-for-achieving-goals.

facilitating career discussions with all employees, not only the high potential ones (where men are often preferred as they are evaluated based on potential over performance). Second, empower employees to own their career plans. By asking powerful coaching questions, you hold them accountable. Get out of their way, and let *their* plan be their plan. As individuals in organizations, speak up and ask for what you want. Share your challenges, your aspirations, and build a plan collaboratively with your manager, mentors, and sponsors.

Male allies are one outlet to facilitate your plan. We believe career game plans have four key elements. The best plans are succinct, focused, and easy to share. They include:

- Our purpose statement: essentially our "why," explaining in one sentence what we are all about.

- Goals: no more than three measurements with a clear timeframe (usually one to three years).

- Competencies: the behaviors, skills, or attributes representing you or what you aspire to build to achieve your purpose.

- Actions: key short-term tasks mapped to goal-fulfilling activities, broken down into manageable steps.

At Pivot Point, we refined our career game plan. Our purpose statement reads, "Develop leaders. Coach women to build winning career game plans. Promote gender equality." This will change over time, as we continue to refine it with our male ally efforts. From this statement, our annual objectives are clear: we have a specific revenue target, a percentage of our business focused on women's leadership and gender equality, and the ambition to publish this book. Competencies important to us achieving our goals and purpose are delegation, presence, and confidence.

We focus our professional development time on building these skills. We align actions each week, using three key tasks to achieve these objectives. We map three bigger objectives, monthly, to the overall annual targets. There are many ways to do this, and time chunking – breaking big efforts into smaller ones – has served us well. For example, once we started setting goals for publishing this book, looking at the project in sections (versus the whole book at once) kept us motivated. It felt more achievable. Do the same with your plans. It is empowering! Let male allies be sounding boards to help you break down your projects into manageable bite-sized chunks.

Whether your organization has a formal individual development plan process or not, writing it down increases your chances of success. If you are a manager, sitting down with every employee at least once a year to document their plan is pivotal and impactful. You learn things you did not know about them, and you are often able to align their work with what they are passionate about. This benefits employee engagement and the business, lowers turnover, improves quality, and boosts productivity.

And, as Jen illustrates, it levels the playing field for everyone to collaborate together, by setting the expectation both genders will document their strategies regularly. This opens the door to learning women's stories, what they want, and where they want to go.

Be the Change You Want to See

While Ghandi initially coined this powerful phrase, it is still relevant today (especially for women seeking male ally support). We must align our beliefs with our aspirations. Men respond to confidence, so fake it a bit until you make it. If we continue to barrage ourselves with self-limiting beliefs and negative self-talk, we will never achieve what we want to achieve. Positive affirmations and modeling success behaviors invites men into the process. They want to champion women who know what they want and have strong presence and confidence.

A plan and positive affirmations drive confidence. Women often employ the negative self-talk reel, or – as some have said – "gremlins." You are not alone if you have these moments or sleepless nights due to self-doubt. Remind yourself these thoughts hold you back and find ways to replace them with positive thoughts. When they express self-doubt, we often ask our clients, "How do you know this is true?" or "Based on what?" They usually have no foundation for the self-limiting thoughts which, if left unmanaged, can become self-fulfilling prophesies.

Affirmations are *also* statements you believe to be true. Some of ours are, "We are leading a movement to promote male allies," "Our work is vital for achieving gender equality," and "We champion everyone to support one another to make the world better for our daughters." When we are having a bad day, reminding ourselves of what we do and why we do it is pivotal. Men can help us flip the negative scripts in our minds, and see the positive attributes in us.

Kim, leader of Integrating Women Leaders Foundation, talked to us about two of the male allies (Tom and David) who have helped her believe more in herself.

> "This is a great story. Tom was the head of the local Chamber of Commerce for many, many years and came to our organization to run one of the business units I was a part of. I was much honored he named me his successor. I was fairly young compared to some of the other folks that could have been named. He really taught me you don't have to be good at everything. I think we put a lot of pressure on ourselves to try and be good at everything and he really gave me permission to focus on the strengths I had. It allowed me to not worry so much about trying to be better at the things that really aren't my gifts. It was incredible."

Kim's story highlights we don't have to be all things to all people. Focus on your strengths, your passions, those skills-and-wills, and align your plan to them. When you confidently convey what you want and focus on, what you are good at, men take note.

Kim has had the support of men throughout her career. This story features David who promoted Kim to her first president position.

> "One of the stories I like to share is about David. He's been very, very successful, highly regarded in the tech space here. We were meeting over a six month period and he wanted to find out what it was going to take to get me. So, I put a list together of what was important for me; for this to be a 'fit.' He hired me on the spot. His trust in me helped me be successful in the role, and subsequently in other president roles. I knew what I wanted, and clearly communicated it. He responded to my confidence."

Chris and David are clear male allies. They responded to Kim's confidence and her leading to leverage her strengths. She understood her limitations, and clearly communicated them to align her plan with success. As a result, she has led and started many businesses in our community. The support of these men accelerated the success.

Another story, from successful entrepreneur and career coaching expert, JT, highlights the power of sharing our story. She dedicated a blog post to male allies.

> "Chris and I met eight years ago when we both became board members for a charity. As the newbies, we decided to pair up and work on a fundraising project together. As we got to know each other over time, (Chris is a talented Private Equity Investor), I found myself reaching out to him regularly for second opinions on business situations. He is one of my favorite people to bounce ideas off of. He never tells me what to do, he just asks me questions to get me thinking deeply. He has a very keen perspective on the insecurities women business owners have and knows how to instill confidence in me. I can't tell you how nice it is to have someone like that in your professional peer group!"

When we talked to Chris, he glowingly shared his experiences, in collaborating with JT, as mutually beneficial. He admires her ability to light up a room when she speaks and how she has grown her business and online presence. Men who see our confidence are motivated to support us.

Be the change you want to see. Rather than waiting for other mentors, coaches, managers to come to you, proactively share your story with those around you who are best equipped to help you succeed. Women who know what they want are far more likely to be successful. With your "why" and career game plan in hand, your chances of success have already increased by 80%. By believing in yourself, and focusing on what you will achieve, male allies are naturally drawn to you.

Women Leader Action Steps

If you're looking to share your story, here are some steps to guide you. You'll find additional actions in the subsequent sections focused on speaking up with him and practicing self-care.

1. What is your "why?" Be sure to reference the questions on page 46.

2. What is your career game plan?

a. What is your purpose statement? Keep this to one succinct sentence.

b. What incremental goals will help you fulfill your purpose? Make sure they are **s**pecific, **m**easurable, **a**ttainable, **r**elevant, and **t**imely (SMART).

c. What competencies (skills, behaviors, attributes) are critical to achieving your objectives? These can be aspirational or build off of your strengths.

d. What are the action steps to achieve your goals? Break down long-term into smaller chunks for the short-term (three to six months).

3. How will you "be the change you want see?"

MALE ALLIES
ASK FOR HERSTORY

Ask Her Questions

Channeling and aligning your strengths with more women who can benefit most from your overall support is step one. Next come actionable tools (from male allies) to cultivate meaningful and powerful impacts on the women in their personal and professional lives. While research estimates females speak on average 13,000 more words than men daily, male voices continue to be heard more inside organizations. Holding 95% of CEO positions and 84% of senior leadership positions, men continue to have a much stronger presence at the decision-making table.[35] Women are often absent when their careers are being discussed. This means men, in most cases, are in a better position to support us than women are. These men can help only if they know what we want and what our stories are. Often, HIStory is the one we hear in the halls of organizations. The difference is: male allies ask for HERstory, knowing we all have something to share.

---

[35] "Women Really Do Talk More Than Men," last modified February 20, 2013, http://www.dailymail.co.uk/sciencetech/article-2281891/Women-really-talk-men-13-000-words-day-precise.html.

Meet Mike and Mike (not the ESPN sports show hosts), men I am privileged to call my male allies. One Mike collaborates with employers to create a great place to work. He describes his knee jerk reaction for men to best help support women as,

> "Just ask. If you're married, just ask your wife 'What can I do today to make your job easier, either at work or at home?' If you're in the workforce and you're managing females, ask them what's getting in their way and how you can help. I think so many times men may feel they can't help because they're a man and they only see themselves as part of the problem. More often than not, they're probably in a really great position to help someone else. For women, I have found – when they know I am there – it helps them feel more supported and more confident to ask for what they want."

Mike two, leader in product development, shared a similar sentiment,

> "A lot of it is just reaching out to women. Look around your meetings, and if there are few women present, ask for a more diverse perspective. I mentor women in preparing them for future positions. Our corporate culture invites men to participate as mentors for women and vice versa."

Mike's motivation is to help *people.*

> "I do not look at it any different than conversations I would have with men. I just want to help. I hate to give myself credit for what I assume most other men, and women, are doing. Real support means avoiding assumptions on someone's capabilities to perform based on the fact they are a man or a woman."

This selfless theme emerges time and time again: not focusing on the difference in genders. Research proves males are more likely to speak up and share needs and aspirations than females. As Mike and Mike shared, sometimes having a man open the door to the conversation helps us feel more comfortable speaking up. Women think sharing their story is being "selfish." Subconscious gender biases still attribute being assertive with "bitchiness." The gender tight rope is still alive. Yet, when men openly invite a woman to share, the perception shifts from self*ish* to self*less*. His selfless act creates a platform for her to speak, leveraging his credibility.

Based on men's positional dominance in most organizations, they are more often in positions of influence. Influence is best shared through asking questions, rather than advising. Male allies shared these questions to start the conversation with women to learn about their stories:

- What do you want?
- Where do you see yourself in five years?
- What are your goals?
- How can I support you?
- What's holding you back?
- What motivates you?
- What will help you achieve your goals?
- What is missing personally and/or professionally?
- What are your strengths?
- How would you describe your dream job?
- What skills do you want to develop?
- What does success look like for you?

These questions are open-ended. They come with positive, genuine intent, inviting women to share. The key words "What" and "How" facilitate a two-way exchange. It is impossible to answer these questions with a concise "Yes" or "No." When a man asks what he can do to help (or what she wants), it sets the expectation she will tell him. Her fears are quieted. By creating a safe place to share, men are privy to information they may never have known. Many shared, joyfully: "I had no idea she wanted that position," or "I didn't realize I could help in such a simple and meaningful way – it felt good to be there for her."

Focus on Her Strengths

Gallup and many other firms have confirmed we are far better by focusing on our strengths over our weaknesses. People prefer working on what they are good at, rather than focusing on where they need to improve. As Stephen

Covey proved in the *7 Habits of Highly Effective People*, when we "sharpen the saw," we're far more likely to succeed and enjoy what we do.[36] It only makes sense men could support women by focusing on their unique strengths.

In our research, we found that females commonly experience self-sabotage and downplay their strengths. In our research with women, they often questioned their abilities and were slow to share their success stories, where men welcomed the chance to be an expert and did not hold back recognizing their accomplishments. Partially due to gender role socialization, partly due to our brain's wiring, women often focus on pleasing others and are more sensitive to relationships and the external perceptions of others. Women focus on blending in with their external environment, and often shared the "disease to please" others. Men, conversely, are more likely to be internally driven, are quick to compete, and are more self-oriented.

As outlined in *The Confidence Code*, the male brain has more neurons focused in the frontal part of the brain (neocortex), which is responsible for rational thought.[37] Women have slightly more activity in the limbic part of the brain, the more emotional center. The findings concluded our wiring is malleable; it is all about teaching our brains how to approach things more rationally and that self-focus in not selfish. Emotions are a strength women bring to the table, with empathy and collaboration skills; yet when overused, these strengths can become weaknesses.

Here are some stories about how men helped women recognize their unique strengths.

Jack, a leader in higher education and a board member of a women's leadership not-for-profit, shared about his aunt's influence.

> "She set high expectations, expected the best, and empowered me. Later in my career, I channeled that to help other women. I remember the first time I picked a woman to help. She was a clerk in the registrar's office at the university, and had great leadership ability. Oh, my goodness! We gave

---

[36]   Covey, *7 Habits of Highly Effective People*, 1-381.

[37]   Kay and Shipman, *The Confidence Code: The Science and Art of Self-Assurance – What Women Should Know*, 1-256.

her an area of leadership. I came alongside ... I wouldn't say as a mentor, but I think a good supervisor provides an equal measure of challenge and support. Lots of time we think, as a mentor, or empowering women, you think of just the support and the encouragement and the empowerment, but I think challenge is an important aspect to it: 'You can do this,' I told her, 'This is a significant project for us. I want you to lead this effort. You can do it. You have the skill set. It may be a stretch for you. When you get too far out there, you always will be supported.'

Depending on the person you're working with, some need a big dose of challenge, some need a big dose of support, but you always have those in equal measure. This empowers people. Down the road, when they begin to see success, it's important to recognize it, to celebrate it, to let other people know this individual did this. This woman became registrar, eventually, then they promoted her to director of enrollment management. By the time I left the school, she was vice president of student development. She became a member on the president's cabinet, and was a senior leader at the university. I think a part of it was recognizing the skills and abilities, providing her with challenges, promoting along the way, and she's just doing terrific. She went on to get a masters, and ultimately a doctorate."

Celebrate her successes. Challenge her to be more. Being a male ally means more than dishing advice or giving a promotion. As Jack's story illustrates, it requires men to see something in the woman she may not see in herself, yet. She may not know her natural gifts or strengths. Jack saw the clerk's ability to lead and aligned the opportunity with her unique talents. He put her in a position to be successful. He did not step away afterwards; instead he provided support throughout the journey. He provided the space to self-discover the path forward and did not take credit for her success.

A director in higher education, Kim shared,

"I think about what kind of leader I want to work for. It's important. Make sure you're thinking about who you want to work for, and who do you have in your life. Whoever your partners are personally and professionally, they need to recognize your strengths, and they need to support you. A great example of this was when I used to get riled up, a former manager would help me step back and look at it. As I would head in that direction, he would say, 'Now let's just break that down.'"

As Kim shares, male allies help us understand what holds us back – what is real, and what is just in our heads. By asking questions, pausing to break it down, and challenging us to be better in the moment, these men inspire the women around them.

Coach Her to Success

It is critical for women to be in a positive place to accept and value coaching. Through overcoming self-doubt and focusing on strengths, male allies help them feel safe. As a Certified Master Coach, I often teach leaders to be coaches. The word "coach" often elicits memories of past sports coaches, or the misperception it is all about giving advice (or even being a therapist). Not at all. Professional coaches help people self-discover. Men are often best suited to do this. As revered leaders and rational thinkers by nature, they can help women remove perceived road blocks.

Fear is a primal emotion crippling people's ability to rationally think through situations. As a coach, creating a safe place for women to be heard and focus forward, rather than backwards, is pivotal. I remember being relieved as a coach to hear *my* coach say, "You do not have to have all the answers. In fact, it's better if you do not know." By parking your assumptions and experiences, you are far more likely to listen for cues and focus her forward.

This may be scary for those seeing something in a woman who does not yet see it in herself. For these common yet dangerous-to-overlook scenarios, we share two of our favorite coaching questions. For those in the throes of self-doubt who do not believe they can self-discover, ask: "What if you *did* know?" or "What if (insert trusted ally here) were here. What would they say?" Women know the answers to their problems. They just cannot see past self-limiting beliefs. They see what they choose to see. What if *you* see something different?

Help them see it, too. She may be choosing the more cautious, "safe" route, thus not seeing what you see. Self-fulfilling prophecies are real perceptions. Our brains tell our bodies what we are capable of and our bodies comply. Any recovering patient or successful athlete will tell you: the hard part was mentally "getting there." When they do, their body delivers accordingly. One of our favorite mantras for women is, "She believed she could, so she did."

Successful entrepreneur, speaker, and influencer, JT reflected on the story of her male ally.

"He didn't treat me like a daughter, he really just coached me. He believed I had my own answers. This was an 'aha' moment for me. It was never a sit down, do this, this and this, it was such a departure from the other male mentors I had had because I did find some just really treated me like a daughter. He looked at me as a peer. To think I might be able to give him value back someday for what he did was a total game changer for me. He is absolutely one of the biggest male allies out there, and if we could clone him it would be a great thing."

For other potential male allies out there, JT indicated,

"What's most important is they understand we're not coming to them to solve our problem. I think there's a common misconception if I'm coming to you, I want you to solve my problem. I don't. Guess what? I'm going to solve my problem. What I'm looking for is a sounding board and what I want you to do is listen to me and if you see something in my mindset that might be myopic or maybe you think is misguided or maybe I should be exploring … ask me a question."

Stories stick in our brains 20 times easier than facts or figures.[38] Knowing HERstory is vital to developing her to be her best possible self. Remind yourself: she doesn't know what she doesn't know. She may not have the awareness about her unique strengths, and she may not have the ability to self-discover her

---

[38] "The Link Between Memory and Stories," last modified January 8, 2015, http://www.anecdote.com/2015/01/link-between-memory-and-stories/.

recipe for success. You can be the difference she needs. Channel the empathy of those who have helped you, root for the underdog, channel your inner "Yoda" and facilitate relationships with those in her network. Once you get her story – what she wants and where she wants to go – be a supporter, challenger, coach, or a connector for her to get there.

Asking for HERstory is best achieved by asking questions, focusing on her strengths, and coaching a woman to success. Here are action steps to build your plan.

Male Ally Action Steps

Male allies listen to the women leaders they support. Male allyship is a journey. Let the questions guide you to begin your journey.

1. Brainstorm questions you will ask a woman to learn more about what she wants. Reference the questions on page 57.
2. List her strengths and consider how you will focus on them.
3. Practice coaching to learn more about her story and how you will help support her.

SECTION FOUR: SPEAK

MALE ALLIES
SPEAK UP *WITH* HER

Meet the Wharton 22s

Successful male allies shared with us it is important for men to offer support through speaking up *with* a woman, not *for* them. The only way she will learn how to stand on her own as a leader is to let her stand on her own! Depending on male support to get her through every barrier creates co-dependence and is not healthy for any relationship. With this principle in mind, let's meet some amazing male allies who speak up *with* women: the Wharton 22s.

They helped us re-orient from "man champions" to "male allies" based on feedback early in the process. When this book was published, "The 22s" was in its fourth full year of operations. It was started by a group of men, at The Wharton School (University of Pennsylvania), who were committed to the cause of gender equality.

As the current president, Sebastian, shares,

> "A lot of the original founders were shaped by personal experiences. They had very strong influential female role models. The more that they have worked their way through the corporate world or even some non-traditional backgrounds, they really saw those role models that they may not have had the same opportunities that they had in those times. The thought was if we can all get together right now and make this a little bit more of a well-known topic that there is this gender

disparity and we can do something about it that we as men actually have a really important role to play. We can leverage our experience here at Wharton. That's really where we came from. The last two years have been a lot around increasing awareness as a club, and the general sense of men's role in this right.

We have a responsibility that we can actually benefit from it. We have publications and events designed to help others identify any implicit biases that we may have or how we see them in the work place. Really trying to understand how others mitigate those and how to be more effective and inclusive leaders. That's where we are. I think every year we shift more from just the general awareness sense to more advocacy and skill development so that we graduate with a tool kit or a skill set to really launch once they get into with workplace."

This group of male allies teaches us all what "good" looks like. It is an excellent example of men collaborating with women with a singular focus to improve gender equality. The mission they have adopted as a group is "To decrease gender disparities and change thought processes that lead to them by encouraging awareness, dialogue, and action on the part of men within the Wharton community."

"The 22s" is a reference to the gender pay gap at the time of the group's inception - one of a number of issues they hope to address. When founded in 2013, the Institute for Women's Policy Research reported a 78% pay gap.

All organizations can learn from what The 22s do well. Best practices include:

- Creating a succinct mission statement focused on gender equality and specific issues the group intends to improve (pay gap, leadership gap, etc.).
- Including men and women in events, publications, and discussions.
- Coining a playful, inclusive name to enlist the support of male allies.
- Developing a strategic, forward thinking leadership team and board.
- Facilitating dialogues about gender equality in companies and communities.

- Supporting mechanisms to facilitate conversations in real-time (T-shirts, social media, slogans, etc.)

Bryce, one of the Wharton 22s board members, elaborated,

> "Speaking up when somebody says something obnoxious in the workplace is a very active form of allyship. I think it's important for people who are comfortable to do that. For those who are not yet at the point of stopping a meeting and saying "That's not appropriate," you can do smaller things. For example, when a woman speaks up in a meeting and somebody else talks over her or takes her idea and starts talking about it as if it were their own, make sure to give credit to the woman.
>
> There are other ways you can signal to your coworkers that you are an advocate for gender equality. If you want to be a super ally, start the equivalent of the 22s in your organization! Or, almost every organization of a reasonable size has some sort of women's group. Just ask the group what you can do to help: "What are some of the biggest issues for you here at this company and how could we help?" These approaches do not require you to stand up in front of your boss and say, 'Don't be a jerk.'"

Once you know HERstory and what she wants, find ways to leverage your voice to speak up. This could be calling out non-supportive behaviors if you feel comfortable doing so, finding ways to redirect the conversation to give her credit for her idea, or the encouragement to take a more active role in the discussion. Asking questions invites sharing thoughts. Seeding an idea (prior to the discussion) to share with others in a meeting can accomplish more than most men realize. The women we interviewed often cited challenges with men speaking for them: "What she really means is…" or inadvertently taking credit for her idea later in a conversation because the male voice was heard last.

Gender norms taught early in life encourage men to speak up for themselves and for women to collaborate. However, when both voices are heard equally, business results improve. Diverse thinking yields more robust solutions in problem solving. It's not that male voices need to be heard less, and females more. Men can act as a microphone for their female counterparts' voices.

They can share the stage and look better doing so. By modeling more inclusive communication, others take note and follow suit. It signals confidence and authenticity, characteristics consistent with effective leadership.

Neal, Wharton 22 leader, shared,

> "If we're focusing on how we're impacting beyond Wharton, I think a lot of it is going to be qualitative in nature. If we based it on being involved in issues, I think that's considered a win. We have had events in the last few weeks where we had a workshop on sexual harassment and sexual assault. It was packed full of people. A lot of those people probably would not have taken an interest before. Now it's part of some people's lives and it's something that people talk about. It's something that people socialize with across the network. I think especially the message whether through official or personal channels, I think that is all very important. What we were speaking about earlier, top down directives to ensure gender equality took place, they have not been effective."

This debate ensued in many of our interviews. Most agreed the top down gender representation standards is not an effective strategy. It hasn't worked. Leaders shared: the belief for equality has to come from within the organization, and all leaders and employees need to buy in fully. An attitude of "We need to have X number of women on our leadership team by Y date" won't drive behavior long term. It reinforces the lose-win mentality when women take men's positions. We need to lower the barriers for men to get involved, as the Wharton 22s demonstrate beautifully.

Steven, one of the Wharton 22s echoed these sentiments.

> "It is important that there are options to display allyship without having to raise conflicts. We gave a bunch of T-shirts that say 'Real Men Stand Up for Women's Equality.' I think that is a way to advertise a message and start a conversation. When someone says, 'Oh, where did you get that shirt and what does it mean?' it creates the opportunity for that to be a conversation. While in a lot of professional places this may

look different, I think in the campus environment there's a lot of value to things like that."

Dan, a Wharton 22 alum, now at a large consumer packaged goods firm, shared,

> "There is a women-in-business-group at my company, and it's only for women. They talk about gender issues and workplace diversity issues. They've had the CEO speak, who's a man, but no men are invited to participate, or even listen in on those conversations. I think there'd be a lot of value for men to be invited to listen. Keeping these groups exclusively to women serves to heighten a guys' perception, like he doesn't know, and it's not his role to ask, and I don't want to say the wrong thing so I'm not going to say anything at all. These subtle things in the workplace make an impact. It's the little things that add up over time. I think there are more men who want to join the fight and support the women around them, but don't know how. They may be nervous they'll say the wrong thing and be embarrassed, or even offend someone."

Finding ways to include men would lower these barriers and broaden the coalition. A message to the men, though - any male ally must act and emphasize publically that he is not there to "save the day" – women have been fighting this fight for generations! Dan underscores another theme from our research: the importance of women opening the door to men and inviting them to participate. If women isolate themselves and not invite men into the conversation, how do we expect things to change if we're continuing to do the same thing ourselves? Women will not solve the pay and leadership gap challenges on their own. Men are often at the top making the decisions! This means male allies are needed to help solve the problem. Through men's positional authority, women are heard.

Be Her Voice When She is Not There

Men are far more likely to be at the table when key decisions are made about the organization. This means they are in the best position to advocate and be her voice when it is not possible for her to attend. That is why knowing her story – what she is good at, and what motivates her – is key. When male allies know what she wants, they can better articulate it to their peers and leaders in a thoughtful, helpful manner. The more men are curious to learn about the women they support, the more successful the mentorship, sponsorship, coaching, advocacy, or management of her career is likely to be.

Kim, a leader in higher education, shares,

> "I've mostly had male bosses. One brought me in as an expert to help create change. So, just recognizing the expertise was important no matter what gender it came from. And then he did lots of little things that made my life easier. If he was invited to meetings, he would take me along. And he would go into the meeting and he would put his coffee cup down and he would leave the meeting. So everybody thought he was there, but basically he had inserted me in his place. It was kind of like passing the torch with a coffee cup. It was as if he was right next to me, and you got the sense everyone knew, 'Oh, that's Shawn. Kim must be taking Shawn's place.'

> I wanted to understand the organization better, so he reached out to six different leaders and set up lunches for me with them. He was thinking that if I talked to them, they would see my expertise and talent. He also set up presentations of the work that I led. He would introduce me, give me credibility, and then let me stand up and do all the rest, and take all the questions. He also gave constant feedback, saying, 'You were a little hard-edged there. Let's see how we could tone this down.'"

Kim's story articulates the need for men to open doors for women. Men's positional influence alone – even if by display of a coffee cup – can serve as a microphone for US. Since women usually must prove their capability more than men, take a page out of Shawn's book: open doors to networking relationships and presentation opportunities and give her the floor to speak (with a nice endorsement to gain interest from the audience). Male allies share their sphere of influence with the woman they choose to mentor, sponsor, or manage through speaking up *with* her, not *for* her.

Erin, author of *The S(He) Says Guide to Mentoring* written in partnership with one of her male allies, Dr. David Borst, shared her expertise.[39]

> "The best advice for men in leadership positions is to ensure that women and everyone in the room are heard—in meetings, through idea sharing, and making the time to meet with them. Women like to be liked and nice, and they rarely talk over men. If a senior level man is in the room – he needs to make sure *all* voices are heard – not just the person with the loudest voice."

Michael, TEDTalk speaker ("Why Gender Equality is Good for Everyone – Men Included"), elaborated on this notion of men speaking up for women and calling out bad behavior.

> "What we have to do is learn to challenge other men. I would ask you, how many times have you been in a meeting where some guy said something stupid and sexist and everybody looks at you with a big eye roll, and we all wonder if she's going to say something. What's likely to happen is some other guy's going to come to her afterwards and say, 'Oh, I'm really sorry that happened, I'm not okay with that.' And what she needs to say is, 'Well, where were you when I needed you in that meeting?'"

What Michael advocates is to include more men in the discussion. His TEDTalk has reached more than 1.3 million people with the premise that men benefit from speaking up for equality. What holds them back often is the negative peer pressure other men project. They do not want to be the only man calling himself a feminist, or leaving the office early to go to his children's activities. Often, due to our gender socialization, men are fearful of the backlash from other men, which prevents them from being the only voice calling out bad behavior when they are in the position to do something about it. In times of doubt, remember the Wharton 22s – "Real men stand up for women's equality."

---

[39] Borst and Albert, *The S(He) Says Guide to Mentoring*, 1.

Social media guru and public advocate for females in business, Dave, realizes some men may not know how to support women, even though they want to. To men on the fringe of becoming male allies, he recommends,

> "I would probably say speak up. There are a lot of men who will be in a networking group, and they'll hear someone say something that may or may not be appropriate and they'll let it ride, let it pass instead of speaking up. There's this thing called 'mansplaining', and you speak slower, as if the woman will understand you better when you're speaking slower. It's actually quite offensive, and not appropriate. You need to understand the culture of dealing with women in business first before you open your mouth. Listen to her. Remember, we have two ears, and one mouth. Listen twice as much as you speak."

Men, if you are afraid, know other men want to speak up, too. They face the same fears. Channel the women you care about, and do it for them. Speak up with them; support them with your voice when they are not there, or when they are there and need an ally to support them.

Mentor Her

Mentoring and sponsoring are different, as we outlined earlier. When a male ally sponsors a woman, he is often being her voice when she is not there, or amplifying her voice as advocates through awareness raising as the Wharton 22s story illustrates. Mentoring is different. Mentors have been in your shoes and done what you want to do. They give advice, share stories, and brainstorm with you. They are notably different from coaches. Coaches promote self-discovery as we outlined prior. Coaches often have not walked the path you want to walk. Mentors have. The best mentors are vulnerable, sharing their lessons learned.

The mentees do not have to make the same mistakes, and they can take advantage of the opportunities discovered, as well. Mentors provide a safe place for a woman to open up and share her fears, ambitions, and what she really wants. Mentees drive the relationship and often set the agenda, identifying objectives for the time together. They own their goals and development plans as a result of the discussions. "Fit" is key. Making sure you have expertise in the areas where she wants to develop proficiency is crucial; connecting her with other resources to explore is also important.

Erin, mentoring author and guru, shares

"Everyone in one's life is a potential influencer and/or mentor. Your friends influence you. Your family influences you. Your mentors and sponsors influence you. And most of all, the people who behave in the exact opposite way you want to behave—the anti-mentors I call them—influence you. Men tend to mentor other men who are 'like' them. As women, we need to ask men to mentor us. They need to be trained on what we want from the mentor relationship, and how we can benefit from sharing their experiences. Mentoring is a two-way street. In my experience, mentors often get just as much out of the relationship as the mentees do."

Our male allies shared the following mentoring best practices:

- Let her drive the relationship. Press her to have clear objectives, yet let her lead discussions.
- Park assumptions. Do not assume you know what she wants. Be curious and learn from her.
- Challenge her and help her overcome her fears (real or unreal).
- Share your story. Be vulnerable and open up about your flaws and challenges and how you overcame them.
- Collaboratively problem solve. Women do not need you to solve their problems. Collaborate with them to solve problems together.

For men wanting to be more active in this effort, we challenge you to learn from the Wharton 22s and mentor talented women you know. Your everyday actions are the bridge to closing the pay and leadership gaps, which benefits everyone.

Male Ally Action Steps

For men looking to be more of a male ally, with the women in mind you want to support, think about how you will mentor or sponsor her.

1. Reflect on the stories from Wharton 22s. Could your organization benefit from an inclusive male ally organization? If you already have an organization focused on gender equality, what best practices would you bring to it? Reference pages 66-67.

2. How will you be her voice when she is not there?

3. If you have done what she wants to do, brainstorm ways to mentor her to success. Reference the best practices on page 73.

WOMEN LEADERS
SPEAK UP *WITH* HIM

Teach Him How You Want to be Treated

This theme emerged consistently in our research. Rather than being treated like a daughter, women want to be a peer – equal to their male allies. The word ally signifies standing beside one another in harmony, where both are equal, even if their power positions are not equal. Since the roles male allies play are far ranging – mentors, sponsors, managers, advocates, coaches, advisors – it is important women know what role they are best suited to play. Rather than shying away from support and guidance, welcome these men into your world. Share your story and invite them to become part of it.

HR leader, Aaron, shared his take on being a male ally.

> "It's someone who will stand up for women's rights regardless of their abilities to stand up for themselves. Many are perfectly capable of defending their rights, but in truth, they shouldn't have to. To quote Spider-Man's Uncle Ben, 'With great power comes great responsibility.' Those in positions of power or authority have the responsibility to do the right thing and push for true equality within their organizations.

> At a previous employer where I served as the HR Director, I constantly supported the two female managers, especially the only one in an operations role. When she wasn't invited to a leadership team meeting, I spoke on her behalf, then

informed her of the meetings. Eventually she was invited to the weekly meetings, rightfully so, and became an equally respected member of the leadership team. The COO even took her under his wing and began grooming her for a promotion."

Aaron's story illuminates the importance of male allies having a natural inclination to speak up when women are not in the room, and are apt to speak up with her when she needs a nudge. By being her voice when she is not there, men are able to help shape successful career paths for the women.

We need to make this easy for men to support us. We need to clearly state how we want to be treated – as a mentee, a coachee, a pupil, a leader, etc. Male allies play a variety of roles, and those who are good at them have demands on their time. Be purposeful and intentional when you ask for his support. Men who know our plans and what we want can share their positional authority with us, acting as a microphone for our stories. By tapping into their voices, we amplify our own. Together, we succeed in speaking up with him, not letting him speak up for us.

Women in our research commented on "bropropriating," men speaking over their female counterparts, taking their ideas, or clarifying what they meant. Do not allow this behavior. Gender socialization cues men to be assertive, dominant, and decisive. All of these encouraged behaviors lead to this "bropropriating" behavior, which is very hurtful to rising women leaders. Everyone should take a stand – this behavior is not okay – and shut it down in the moment. As women, saying, "Let me clarify; what I meant to say was…" or "I have a different point of view …" gets the attention of male allies. Be direct and you are more likely to be heard. If you do not feel comfortable doing this yourself, entrust a male ally with your challenge, and ask for his support. Let his voice amplify yours by dismissing bad behavior in the moment. By continuing to support "bropropriating" behavior, we teach men it is acceptable to treat us this way.

Ask for What You Want

Start the dialogue with intentionality. Male allies encourage women to speak up and share what they want. We are gender socialized to be more emotional and less confident. The male allies we interviewed admitted to feeling overwhelmed and frustrated in emotionally-laden conversations. They indicated that they did not know what to do when working with less direct, less confident women, thus defaulting to advice, or even worse, rescue mode. Tell him what you want, and ask for his support to get there. Get to the point quickly, and ask questions to facilitate his thinking. Be clear and assert yourself confidently. Tell him you do not want the answers, and he will respond positively to your ask.

In Linda Babcock's book, *Ask for It*, she cites men are four times more likely to negotiate than women.[40] Babcock found we are fearful of speaking up and asking for what we want. Interestingly, when women negotiate on each other's behalf, they have more successful outcomes than men. This proves we are equally skilled at negotiation.

We have natural strengths in seeking win-win solutions through collaboration, but we need to have a safe place to ask for it. Women in our research indicated negotiating for others helped them feel more confident. If speaking up is hard for you, think of someone you care about and channel them, asking, "What if (insert amazing person) were here, what would they say?" or "If I ask for it, how will this benefit others?"

Dolly, bias expert, shares her story about her PhD advisor and male ally, Max.

> "Max has been incredibly egoless in sharing his credit with me and other women throughout his career. The social science says men tend to interrupt us without realizing they're doing it; they tend to overtake credit without realizing they're doing it; they tend to forget where ideas originated without realizing they're doing it. Max is the opposite of that. He very consciously strives to not do those things. I think he's built up a habit where he also just doesn't even consciously do them. And when he does mess up, he deals with it and apologizes for it."

> She continues, "He is also very creative. He's a negotiations professor, so he's really good at creating win-win solutions, and he's been really creative at seeing opportunities to match

---

[40] Babbock, *Ask for It*, 1.

people. For example, 'I know Dolly's interested in education, and maybe we can craft this one particular speaking engagement so that it can focus on education, and then it will be a really high-profile thing for her and it wouldn't be detracting from her underlying goals because it would be focused on the thing she's passionate about.'

He doesn't make assumptions. I'm a mom with two kids. He doesn't assume that because I'm a mom with two kids I'm not willing to do certain things. Now, do I often say 'No' to things he invites me to? Yes. I probably say 'No' far more than I say 'Yes.' But he also doesn't take that personally. He lets me make the decision rather than assuming I'm a mom with two kids so why ask, or being discouraged because I've said no three times in a row.

He does a lot of sharing accomplishments when we're not in the room. He's very vocal in championing his female coauthors to other people. I hear from other people all the time - people I'm meeting for the first time, who I wouldn't think would know who I was – 'Oh, Max was here last year giving a talk, and he was talking all about you.' That's really intentional on his part. I don't think it just kind of happens to come to mind.

He actively does this with his male coauthors as well, but it's particularly impactful for the females that he's always out there talking about us to others, looking for opportunities when he's talking to others. As people start asking questions – 'Is she movable? Doesn't she have a family?' – he shuts that down, saying, 'Why don't you let her answer that? Why are you asking me that? Assume she's movable until she tells you she's not.'"

We learn two successful strategies from Max and Dolly's story. First, women can leverage male allies to find common ground and create win-win solutions. Men often cited enormous benefits of allyship when they knew their gifts had a positive impact. Second, male allies shut down bad behavior and gender assumptions very quickly. They do not speak up for you, they speak up with you and provide a forum for you to communicate your objectives. These men do not assume to know what you want. They ask you what you want.

Laszlo, a former Wharton 22, a male ally group we featured earlier, has spoken at organizations focused on gender equality (including Google).[41] He explains his concern for men telling her story.

> "We don't want to tell that story (about how we've had an impact) for someone. To the extent that we've changed someone's life or their experience - that's really their story to tell. Much of our focus (as male allies) - from a philosophical perspective - is: 'how do we change our behavior?', 'how do we re-examine the way we look at the world?' Hopefully that will have an impact for others, but it's really about personal responsibility more so than getting credit for helping."

What Laszlo and the Wharton 22s share is a common purpose: it is not about taking credit. It's about being a part of changing the thinking that leads to more positive behaviors. This requires women to speak up and ask for male allies to support them.

In *How Remarkable Women Lead*, we learn there are five traits of remarkable female leaders – meaning, framing, connecting, engaging, and energizing.[42] The stories are astounding. The book provides tools for women to discover what they want and where they find meaning and happiness. It also helps them align expectations, connect with purpose, speak up, and tap into their natural energy. We can tailor this framework to our use. We believe in leveraging existing tools, and have aligned our strategies to apply this proven model seamlessly to male allies. When men are aware of how they can contribute the most value, we're able to speak up with him, and practice self-care.

The authors of *How Remarkable Women Lead*, Joanna Barsh and Susie Cranston call on women to "stand up, speak up." They highlight the fear of being found out, of not being good enough. For those familiar with Amy Cuddy's infamous "imposter syndrome," you know this phenomenon haunts

---

[41] "Laszlo Syrop & Ashley Wells: 'Wharton 22s' Talks at Google," last modified September 29, 2016, https://www.youtube.com/watch?v=a2mvNx1pcI0.

[42] Barsh and Cranston, *How Remarkable Women Lead*, 173.

women and often holds them back.[43] Instead, Barsh and Cranston offer lessons through interviews with successful women:

1. "It may not come naturally, but you must speak up to be counted."
2. "Find a valued way to contribute."
3. "Sometimes, it takes a wrong turn to discover your voice."

With practical activities to practice, they are helping us understand: not speaking up is accepting being ignored. It's okay to stumble, but think of where you can add the most value based on your strengths, and your voice is more likely to be heard. This is especially true if strong male allies are cheering you on. It's okay to take risks. Again, gender norms teach women to be more risk averse than men. If you never fail, you're not trying hard enough. Asking, "What's the worst that could happen?" helps us overcome the fear of failure. Speaking up is a risk, yet not speaking up is a bigger one. You'll never get what you want if you do not ask.

Draw Clear Boundaries

Male allies highlighted the importance of expectation-setting and having clear objectives. Once they understand their role and how they can help, they need to be held accountable. Emotional intelligence was another powerful theme in our research, where men noted the importance of being level-headed and listening vs. being drawn into emotions. Emotion drives us, and it is important our purpose is based on some emotion. However, emotions are better when managed in healthy discussions with men. This notion of drawing clear boundaries for them – what you are missing, and what you want from them specifically – is pivotal.

Once we have started the dialogue with our male allies, shared our story, taught him how we want to be treated, and asked for what we want, we need to clearly state our expectations for the relationship. If your male partners wonder what role they are playing in your career, or what impact they are having on you, it is your job to let them know. Assuming they see what you see is a misstep. I made this mistake early in my career with a senior VP mentor I was lucky to

---

[43] "Your Body Language May Shape Who You Are," last modified October 1, 2012, https://www.ted.com/talks/amy_cuddy_your_body_language_shapes_who_you_are.

have. He was one of the top ranking leaders of our organization, and asked me in one of our meetings, "What do you want from this relationship?" Yikes. I did not have an answer. Shame on me for wasting his time and not having a clear objective. I took that feedback and began writing him monthly updates with key bullet points on what I had accomplished, where I was thriving, and where I was struggling. He could quickly prepare for our meeting reading through my notes, and it opened up the dialogue purposefully.

Learn from my mistake. Our male allies are busy. While they love to give, they deserve to know how they can specifically help and the impact they are having. Give them a window into your world, and let them know where their support made a difference. This encourages more men to get involved and build stronger relationships with existing male allies. This is a multiplier effect for you and other women.

Male ally advocates, Brad and David, authors of a powerful mentoring book, shared,

> "It is important that women affirm their male allies. When he demonstrates empathy, champion him for being 'that guy.' As we write in our book, 'that guy' is a male ally that really gets it, the one who understands that as women enter leadership positions at work, organizations are more effective and collegial. Women need to be allies for their male allies."

Rachana, founder of "The Corner of the Court Project" is passionate about women sharing their stories of male allies.[44] She builds off of Brad and David's points. In her research, she found when women provide feedback to men specifically about how their support has impacted them positively, the perception of effectiveness climbs.

> "I asked male allies, 'If a woman told you your behavior was making an impact on her in a positive way, would it help improve your assessment of effectiveness?' They nodded their heads vigorously. 'Absolutely!' they told me. They then very thoughtfully continued by saying anything to help them see

---

[44] "Women's Stories of Outstanding Male Allies & Champions," last modified July 28, 2017, http://www.cornerofthecourt.com/.

there is visible progress, affirmation that they are saying the right things, and reinforcement of specific behaviors that have helped advance the cause, would greatly build their confidence in their efforts."

She continues,

"This is why the intentional conversation is so important. It is not to be confused with a 'pat on the back;' rather, it offers a discussion about those specific and measurable behaviors that have made a positive difference. Then, men can internalize the behaviors, commit to replicating them, and enlist other champions by sharing their stories and tactics. I realize it sounds simple, but this call to action really is easy. For women and others who have been supported by a champion at some point in their careers: just tell them."

Rachana's research, blogs, and her "Corner of the Court" platform allows women to create an intentional acknowledgement to their male allies, and to inspire others by sharing how a male ally has helped them. It is a public way of giving men the confidence in their behaviors and illustrating specific stories and examples to which everyone can relate. She believes sharing such stories of success is important to everyone, as we work side-by-side.

JT, founder of WorkIt Daily, elaborates,

"Ladies, let's teach them how to be our male allies. Let's reward them by being great female allies at the same time. Give them an incentive to want to do this. I think that I'm really lucky in that I'm married to a guy who's always been my ally. He's always wanted that, and I have always wanted to do the same for him. It works well when you both coach each other on what that means and how you do it.

As women leaders, we can train and teach all men how to be allies. Certainly, put them on a pedestal when you do find one, really recognize them. Don't keep them a secret."[45]

---

[45] "Work It Daily," last modified July 29, 2017, https://www.workitdaily.com/.

JT underscores the importance of public recognition. Show others what "good" looks like. By being allies for our male allies, they are more motivated to support us and others. When they do not know the impact they are having, they can become discouraged and feel unappreciated. Help them see what you see. Give them a window into your world, share your story, and let them be a platform to speak up and amplify your own voice.

Women Leader Action Steps

For women looking to speak up with him, here are some steps to guide you.

1. What role do you want your male allies to play? How will you teach them how you want to be treated?

2. How will you leverage their voices to ask for what you want? How will you speak up *with* them, and shut down those who try to speak up *for* you?

3. How will you draw clear boundaries for your male allies? How will you recognize good behavior from them?

SECTION FIVE:
WORK-LIFE

WOMEN LEADERS PRACTICE SELF-CARE

Work-Life Balance is Impossible

Work-life balance is a challenge and it is not only a "woman's problem." Perfect balance is not possible for working families. In our work with women's leadership groups, our survey data revealed the top challenge for the overwhelming majority of members is balancing work and life. Women continue to bear the brunt of the household labor from parenting, to housework, to errand running, although studies indicate men are participating more in household labor. As the 2016 Bureau of Labor Statistics for the U.S. reports, women still spend more time on household labor averaging 2 hours and 15 minutes per day, while men average 1 hour and 25 minutes per day.[46] A ratio of 62/38 women to men, which becomes even worse when you factor in time caring for children and others. Women have 50 fewer minutes a day to spend on self-care, whether that is family, workout, or career time.

There is still this notion of "how does she do it all?" which implies she is not doing something, or that she is dropping the ball somewhere. Accepting there are some good weeks and some bad weeks, some good days and some not so good days, is okay. It's not always rainbows and sunshine. Upon reflection, women shared with us that, once they accepted work and life are more like a

---

[46] "American Time Use Survey," last modified December 20, 2016, https://www.bls.gov/tus/charts/household.htm.

teeter totter than a perfect balance, they began to see more of the good and focus on what drives them versus what depletes them.

According to the National Alliance for Caregiving and the AARP, from 1997-2015 the number of businesses increased by 51%. Of that increase, 74% of the companies are women owned.[47] When people feel trapped in jobs without flexibility, they self-select out of rigid corporate America to start a business. As bread winners and caregivers, it is hard to find time to do it all well. According to this study, 24 million females care for others 25+ hours/week. In fact, they leave the workforce on average 12 years to care for children and relatives. These are smart, talented women who could bring tremendous value to our economy and to organizations, yet society accepts – and even encourages- opting-out of their careers. We make assumptions about the preference to be at home or need to be with the children, whereas the same assumptions are not applied to working men. With the challenge of managing work and life, women often feel exhausted, having no time to care for themselves.

A male ally in the technology space advocates for females in his industry. Jeff blogs and manages a group called the Indy CIO Network. He shared an insight he had about women leaders:

> "Of the 175 members, only 20 are women, and usually only one comes to our monthly networking event. I have asked why they don't come to networking events, and they often say they are tired of being the only woman in the room. I asked if they ever get used to it, and they say they really do not. They are exhausted at the end of the work day, and lack the energy required to be the only woman in the room. So, we organized a dinner with the 20 women and I was the only man present. I sought their feedback and we had a very open discussion.
>
> I realized what they were talking about first hand, being the only man with all women. I get it, now. They shared that sometimes they really do just want to talk about shopping and children, and men do not always want to talk about these topics. I am happy to talk about my grandkids, not sure about

47   "Caregiving in the U.S.," last modified June 2015, http://www.aarp.org/content/dam/aarp/ppi/2015/caregiving-in-the-united-states-2015-report-revised.pdf.

shopping, but we are all human, and have more in common than we realize."

Jeff's story illustrates how difficult it is for men to understand what it's like to be the only woman in the room. Most industries and professional groups are male-dominated, and men are accustomed to being around people like them – men. As females, we need to think about it from a male perspective. To enlist male allies' support, help them understand what it's like to be you. We don't want to play victim here, yet sharing challenges about managing work and managing life is real. Be human, and open up to them. As Jeff shows us, they care, and they want to support us. Jeff is actively seeking more women to join his networking group. He has worked for several female managers in his career and has advocated for women in leadership.

Jeff is actively them gain access to senior roles in technology, and he does it because he knows the diversity of thought makes the team – and business – better. Yet, even as a vocal male ally, he struggles: how can he help? Male allies don't know what they don't know. We must share our story, and help them understand how they can best support us.

Kristin, senior business leader and president of her organization's women's council, shares,

> "For me, what was most important for my self-care was finding a good partner. One of the things he loves the most about me is my success. Without that, it would be incredibly hard to be successful because I would constantly be battling how my personal life fit with my professional life if I had to be a different person at home than I am at work. It gives me a lot of joy to know that what makes me successful at work and what makes me who I am as a woman and a leader is something that my husband loves and values and doesn't feel threatened by. I think that's really important. In fact, unsolicited, he'll share those are some of the characteristics – my independence and my drive and my passion – that initially attracted him to me. I'm very thankful for that. Having my husband in my corner has made it easier for me to open the door to other male allies. I've been given tremendous responsibility and had the career I have had because of their belief in me."

Kristin helps us see how women feel the personal and professional tug of war at times. For her, having supportive male allies at home and at work who know who she is and what she stands for is important. She does not have to show different sides of herself at home and at work, feeling conflicted. She gets to be who she authentically and genuinely is in both parts of her life, which makes her whole.

Accept that while work-life balance may be impossible, practicing self-care is not. We found women do not make time to do this nearly as much as they should. The long-term effects of not practicing self-care is detrimental to our wellness, careers, and families.

You Can Only Make Others as Happy as You are Yourself

When you are exhausted, you do not have the energy to give to others. Remind yourself you are unable to have the energy you need to give to others if you are not practicing self-care. This is why your "why" is critical. Your "why," what fuels you, must be fueled by you. Your "why" transforms how you think and feel, positively impacting the world around you. Women where I coach and facilitate workshops note they are exhausted by the expectations they put on themselves and that society places on working mothers. You cannot give to others when you are empty yourself. As primary caretakers, remind yourself to fill your tank so you can fill the tanks of others.

Vice President of Product Development, Carrie, inspires us with her personal story of making time for her purpose.

> "In 2014, I became reacquainted with the once dreaded half marathon. I had run the 500 Festival Mini Marathon each year from 2007-2009, but it was not as enjoyable and the training was difficult. Once I became a mother, going out for a run was a chance for 'me' time. But it was so much more than that. It was an outlet to digest my thoughts – almost a form of meditation.
>
> Much to my delight, my oldest sister signed up to run with me – her first half marathon. Initially, we set out to do this as a fitness challenge. But before training officially began, our half marathon quest suddenly took a turn to be so much

more when my sister's friend, Connie (aka 'Wonder Woman'), was diagnosed with cancer. From that point on, I had a purpose and focus. Something to keep me going. Something much more powerful than a fitness challenge. Sadly, Connie's journey came to an end along with the lives of others whom I thought about during my training runs.

Then, in November 2014, just days after running in the Indianapolis Monumental Half Marathon, the world stopped turning during my car ride home from work. That evening, I learned my mom – the lifeblood of my family and all around amazing woman – was diagnosed with stage four lung cancer that had metastasized to other areas in her body. My family – who is my everything – joined even closer together to fight this awful disease alongside my mom.

From that point forward, when I ran, it was for my mom. I dedicated my races and every mile of each race to her. And while we had success with a few courses of treatment, at the end of each high was a low – the cancer eventually grew smarter. Unfortunately, the cancer and side effects of the treatments got the best of her and she passed on June 30, 2016. She's in peace and comfort as she looks down from above on all of the lives she had touched. Since 2007, I have run 11 half marathons (eight since becoming a mother). I haven't trained for one since my last race in April 2016, though I still workout each week and participate in 5K races."

We happened to sit by Carrie at a networking event, and hear her story. She shared a photo of her daughter with arms open wide at a finish line. Her mantra – "I do it for me, I do it for my family, I do it for my children" – is such a powerful example. Carrie's story underscores the importance of channeling your passions, prioritizing time to fulfill your passions, and showing your children what "good" looks like. Carrie's courage, dedication, and her daughter's open arms illustrate a compelling message for us to follow. This is what good self-care looks like. If something makes you happy, motivates you, or inspires you, prioritize it. Make the time for your "why." When women get away from their purpose – personally and/or professionally – it is a dangerous situation. Their energy continues to plummet, leaving them physically and emotionally unwell.

A mentor of mine enjoys singing. Having a business, a working husband, and two young boys, she had not made much time to sing. She realized her energy was lacking, and asked her husband for two nights a week to sing. He agreed, and her energy rebounded quickly, giving her a healthy release and the ability to bring her energetic best self to her children (and renewed energy in her business). She had to fuel her passion for it to power her in return. It's not selfish to make time for yourself. It will make you a better mother, partner, leader, and employee. You will be better for those you care about.

We must model the behaviors we want to see from others. John, diversity advocate and experienced male ally, reveals,

> "On a personal side, I go back to my relationship with my wife. We met when we were in our mid-20s. I've been socialized over the last 35 years of our marriage to help with everything from cleaning to cooking to running kids back and forth and creating work/family balance that allows her – in many cases – to do what she wants to do. That takes sacrifice by both parties. I think there is a personal perspective based on how we are socialized."

For women looking to engage male allies, be aware of their backgrounds. Just because they have not been exposed to diversity or strong women leaders does not mean they cannot figure it out. They can learn, and you might need to guide them a bit more. Meet them where they are. Help them help you. In the words of Beyoncé, "Who's there to save the hero after she saves the world?" John shared this lyric with us, and we thought how fitting it would be to include it here. This is precisely what we mean by practicing self-care. As women, we want to believe we can do it all, but the reality is we cannot do it *alone*. We need to enlist the support of men or we will end up saving everyone but ourselves. Thus, unable to continue to support others. If not for you, do it for those around you.

Shauna, a senior leader, elaborated,

> "I'm a little self-critical. It can limit me from being the best version of myself. But there are small wins I can have along the

way that make me feel like I'm a better version of myself than if I didn't do those things. Each week, I have a blowout hair appointment that helps me refuel so I can be the best version of myself for others. It's my hour therapy session with my hair dresser who I've been going to every week for five years. She's a friend of mine.

I can say anything or I can sit in the chair and not say a word because I don't feel like talking. We have that kind of relationship. I walk out of the chair and I feel like I look the way I want to look. And I'm feeling accomplished and less self-critical."

This is what good self-care looks like. Take a page out of Shauna's and Carrie's books. They make time for themselves and their lives improve as a result of the investment.

Give Intentionally

The most important word to practicing good self-care is "No." If we say "Yes" to everything, we are saying "No" to ourselves. It feels good to say "Yes," yet there are negative consequences of using it for everything. We can easily forget our passions and purpose and miss what is best for us (or others around us). By ensuring we say "Yes" to the right things, our giving is aligned with our "why." When we give intentionally, women are far more likely to attract positive male allies.

Diane, executive coach and wellness expert, explains self-care.

"Self-care is essential for balancing work and life. We need to be our own best friend at the times that matter the most. From those 2:00am-cannot-sleep moments to negative thoughts creeping in day-to-day, self-care coupled with self-compassion is critical. I no longer watch the news. I found it to be too disruptive to my mental stability. Based on my experiences, I now help clients set boundaries. It's all about saying no to things you do not want, and choosing to say yes when you want to say yes. I have a mantra – 'I let balance come and go.' For example, my husband does the majority of our household duties – cleaning, home schooling, etc. – and he does a better job in some ways than I did at home. He does not get sucked into the emotions. There are very few days that I do not want to be at work. If I do not want to be there, I know it's time to make a change."

Diane shows us what "good" looks like, and how – by saying "Yes" to the right things – we can say "Yes" more often to others. It is only fitting we conclude with one of the strongest male allies, Adam Grant. Adam is author of *Give and Take*[48] and *Originals*,[49] both compelling reads to shake up our views of giving and original thinking. Being a fan of his work, we reached out to Adam when writing this book. Knowing he is incredibly busy, we thought: what is the worst that could happen? As a genuine and intentional giver, Adam politely declined an interview, but gave us five names of men and women passionate about male allies.

All responded, and this book is far better with their input. From J.T. O'Donnell's blog reaching 450+ likes, 50+ comments, and 60+ shares on LinkedIn, to meeting famous authors, experts, and speakers at the forefront of male allyship, Adam's support paved the way for other men to follow our movement and engage in the content.[50] It's a great story of how "giving intentionally" helps everyone.

In his book *Give and Take*, Adam Grant outlines three types of people – givers, matchers, and takers – and how each behavior correlates to success. He finds some Givers – those who are "door mats" accommodating other's demands – can be the least successful. They forget themselves in the process. However, Givers are among the *most* successful when they give intentionally. Matchers are semi-successful: giving to get. Takers are often the least successful long-term. Their self-serving intentions are often easily perceived by others (who then take advantage) around them.

---

[48]   Grant, *Give and Take: Why Helping Others Drives Our Success*, 1.

[49]   Grant, *Originals: How Non-Conformists Move the World*, 1.

[50]   "Do You Have a Male Ally," last modified June 6, 2017, https://www.linkedin.com/pulse/who-your-favorite-male-ally-j-t-o-donnell.

Giving in strategic ways aligned with our strengths, passions, and purposes is key. When we give to others, we need to ensure it is the best use of our "give" and energy. Simply responding to the needs of others is dangerous. If you are a good networker, for example, find ways you can connect those in your network with others who will benefit from those acquaintances.

The results will fuel you to give more. For me, it would be a big mistake to offer to perform detail-oriented tasks for someone. I am far better at giving through writing, speaking, or sitting down one-on-one with someone to discover what's next in their career path. This means aligning your gives with your passions and strengths, rather than saying "Yes" to everything. If you say "Yes" to everything, you are saying "No" to a lot of things.

Women who understand the importance of self-care shared these additional strategies with us:

- Outsource activities you do not have the skill or will to do. We hired a housekeeper to clean our house once a month, and have enjoyed the ROI of having more time with my family, and more energy and time to do the really important things professionally and personally.

- Say no to FOMO (fear of missing out). Prioritize what is important for you to be happy, overcoming the fear of missing out on the wrong things. Social media is a big influence here. Before you say "Yes," remember it means "No" for something else that may be important. Do say "No" if something does not drive your happiness.

- Get more sleep. Adults need seven to nine hours of sleep per night. Unless you have a genetic mutation, this means you. Very few women we coach get the required seven hours of sleep per night, which is dangerous for their health.

- Implement the 80/20 rule. Make sure 80% of your energy is aligned with your "why". Twenty percent is for the other stuff (routine tasks, things only you can do, etc.).

- Show compassion for others. Find everyday-ways to genuinely, meaningfully help others. Giving fuels our energy.

- Practice gratitude. Journal what you are grateful for each day. Intentionally choose to focus on what is good in your life.

- Have a plan. If you do not know what you want and where you're going, you will fall victim to others deciding for you.

Women Leader Action Steps

As we conclude our final strategy for women looking to engage male allies, remember to start the dialogue with the WIIFM (what's in it for men), share your story, and speak up with him. As you practice self-care, we share these steps to guide you:

1. What are the critical self-care activities fueling your "why" (skill/will)? How much time have you set aside, per week, to practice self-care?

2. What will you say "Yes" to more often? What will you say "No" to more often to make time for your "why"?

3. How will you give more intentionally?

MALE ALLIES
DO THE FAIR SHARE

Be "All In"

Our research on male allies revealed a strong group of supporters actively, spreading the message of equal roles for everyone. Whether this was from a parent, caregiver, spouse, or partnership perspective, a final theme emerged: doing the fair share together.

We had the privilege to speak with former NPR and CNN reporter and male ally, Josh Levs. Josh is author of the book, *All In: How Our Work-First Culture Fails Dads, Families, and Businesses - And How We Can Fix It Together.*[51] He left a successful career at CNN to work on issues of gender equality full-time. He shared his big message with us.

> "It's about all of us helping each other. There's this false idea the problem is that society is unfair to women, and men should be helping women in order to be nice. That's a nice idea, but it misses the other half of the point, which is that we all benefit from gender equality at home and at work. We all need to help each other."

---

[51] Levs, *All In: How Our Work-First Culture Fails Dads, Families, and Businesses - And How We Can Fix It Together*, 1.

Josh went on to explain how gender socialization impacts these behaviors.

"Guys are trained, from the time we are boys, not to talk about a lot of this stuff. So many guys I've interviewed and spoken with, as I travel around and give speeches, share how afraid they are to talk about gender equality. They think if they start to talk about it, someone will say to them, 'Oh, you are a man in a patriarchal society, who are you to talk about these issues?' I always say my experience shows that it's the opposite. It's not just about supporting women; we also need women to support men as caregivers."

Josh's passion was sparked with a series of interviews he conducted on fatherhood.

"At CNN, I was a fact checker. At the time I became a father, I was correcting politicians and presidents, and I started doing some reports about fatherhood. I interviewed groups of dads on the air. We had normal conversations, the kind I have with my friends who are fathers. We talked about how some felt as stay-at-home dads, or stress at work, how much they were upset to work so much because they missed things at home, and how they differed from their fathers. The first time I aired segments of me interviewing other dads the responses we got were crazy huge, like off the wall huge. It was the number one thing on the CNN Newsroom blog.

I got calls from media wanting to interview me about being a dad who interviews dads. I was like, 'What's going on here?' That's how I came to understand that no one knew the truth about dads. They only saw these stereotypes. They really believed these stereotypes of dads as lazy and uninterested. That's just factually not the deal. I took my fact checking lens and I turned that to fatherhood. I started looking at studies showing what's really going on with modern dads and how we're just as involved and working just as hard as moms, and having our own struggles because we have all these pressures on us to stay at work more and more and more when we really want to be home more and more."

Josh's passion ignited even more with the birth of his daughter.

"When my wife was pregnant with our third child we realized that I would be needed at home for caregiving after her birth. I knew this was totally normal because I was reporting on this stuff. Dads do caregiving, now. The policies at CNN were ridiculous, but – sadly – representative of what a lot of places have. The net result of the policies at CNN was that anyone could get ten paid weeks to care for their new child except a guy who got his own wife pregnant, a traditional biological father. Anyone. If I put my daughter up for adoption and someone else I work with, even a guy, adopted her, he would get ten paid weeks.

Or if I had a same sex domestic partner and he adopted a baby. I didn't even have to adopt a baby, I could still get ten paid weeks. Anyone except a traditional dad. I went to the company, and said, 'Look, this has got to be an oversight. There's no way you meant to exclude the possibility that a dad in a traditional scenario might be the caregiver, might be caregiving.' They responded, 'Oh, that's interesting. They said put it in writing,' but then nothing happened. Months went by. Then my daughter was born prematurely in an emergency. My wife had very severe preeclampsia and they had to induce. Still no answer from work about whether I was going to get the time off.

Then, 11 days later I was home holding my four pound preemie and caring for my sick wife and my two boys. I asked, 'Look, I have to know. Do I have more time off?' Because a guy like me could only get two weeks. That's when they said "No." I ended up taking legal action. I filed a charge with the Equal Employment Opportunity Commission. That got a ton of publicity and that led to all these experiences that I've had ever since. Ultimately, the company revolutionized its policy and made it much better for everyone. CNN will tell you the same thing I did. They've said this publicly, and it was a win-win for them as well. It is a pure win when you have better policies, because you keep good people. It costs so much money to replace an employee."

As Josh outlines, the more organizations support male employees as fathers, the more likely they are to retain good staff. Giving them the space to bond with their children early decreases absenteeism long-term and boosts productivity upon return from paternity leave. As you will see in section five, this strategy for male allies becomes practicing self-care for females. Having spoken at many gender equality or women's affinity groups recently, every survey of women's needs in the last year has one key theme at the top – work-life balance. It's not a problem men vocalize, yet, as Josh shared in our interview,

> "Work-life conflict is unnatural. The two things that come most naturally to human beings are working and loving. We build huts. We gather food. We work by nature, and we love our families by nature. If you just leave human beings alone, we're going to work and live and it's going to feel natural.
>
> It's not conflicted. The reason we have so much work-life conflict is that our work culture was built in the Mad Men era in the 1950s after the war and society was going through this whole new time. There was this ideal being instilled, a lot of effort to push the women who had gone to work during World War II to stay home and have lots of babies. This new ideal being created that was very strictly gendered of what it means to be successful, what it means to be the superpower America, what it means to be an American corporation, what it means to be a man. Especially a white middle class man. This whole idea that the man works and makes the money, and the woman stays home and raises the babies. That is how our workplace was designed. It was designed with work-life balance in mind. The balance was the man works all the time, and the woman has the life all the time. The idea of one person existing in both places, at work and at home, is anathema to that culture.
>
> As I continue to share my story, people are shocked to learn we're the only developed nation, almost the only nation at all, with no paid maternity leave. No one ever talks about why. The reason we don't have any paid maternity leave is that we have institutional sexism. The belief is she's a woman. Who needs her money? Men make money. There's supposed to be a man who makes all the money, because that's what men do,

and the woman stays home without money. The net result is that we have no system in this country to make sure a baby can have a parent at home and food on the table for at least a block of weeks.

To change this dynamic of work and life in conflict, which negatively impacts our children, Josh offers this. "The number one thing is absolutely to start talking about this stuff in a public way, both at work and at home and out in the community. The struggles of fathers have been taking place in the shadows. That is severely damaging. People don't know that dads want to be home and are very involved. There are all these bosses out there who genuinely believe women do everything at home anyway. They believe the stereotype. We must change this misperception by speaking up together – men and women."

We could not have said it better than Josh. Josh's story illustrates many challenges in managing work and life in healthy, balanced ways. Where work and life can coexist and we can be the parents we want to be. To prioritize motherhood over fatherhood creates a falsehood. It polarizes parenthood into two unachievable halves. It limits our ability to raise children who see both parents equally and not feel the stress of both trying to fit into prescribed gender roles. In addition to what Josh offers, here are some other proven strategies our male allies offered for companies and managers looking to attract and retain top-talent:

- Offer more than flexible time. Encourage employees to take it.
- Openly communicate the paternity and maternity policies to avoid surprise exits by otherwise all-star employees.
- Align cultural values with work and life management, setting the expectation unhealthy, unsustainable behaviors are not acceptable.

Employees need to speak up as Josh shows us and be "all in," advocating for paid parental leave and fair treatment across genders for equal opportunity to parent. When confronted with a gender inequity situation, ask yourself, "If I were the opposite gender, would they treat me this way?" If the answer is no, it's your duty to call out bad behavior in the moment. If you say nothing, you are saying it is okay.

Divide and Conquer

Fearless senior sales leader, Jen, shared similar sentiments to Josh on balance.

> "Balance is a funny word because it implies there's some semblance of organization. Usually, it's just organized chaos. With my recent promotion, my husband and I did have a conversation about the logistics, and it seemed we didn't have to change a ton. I just need his support of us being more proactive about our schedules. We use a shared app to coordinate our family calendar. So if there's something that comes up where one of us can't pick up the kids, we just use that family calendar to plan the logistics of it.
>
> It saves us from spending our time talking about the logistics of our children. We can talk about other things versus who's doing pickup and drop-off, or how many times one has done one or the other. When I made the decision to pursue the promotion, there was not a moment of wavering with him about going for it. He is extremely supportive, and what made me feel really safe in going for something where I wasn't sure about travel and the impact to us, he was open to that. It's not as though there's some finite risk involved. It's much more like, 'Why would you not give this a shot? You're going to be great. Go for it.'"

Now, *that's* "all in!" Jen finds when she and her husband coordinate calendars in advance, she can communicate it proactively to her team, and manage expectations based on her family's boundaries. She and her husband divide and conquer, picking up and dropping off equally, as well as managing household tasks. When Jen took on the new role, she committed to being home with her children 3-4 nights during the week. She made sure her manager and team were aware of the commitment.

When we asked Jen about being home less frequently in the evenings, she replied, "Absolutely not, that's not what I want. I can do my job and be home most nights. We just have to have a plan." When men are "all in" as husbands and fathers, it creates a safe place for women to speak up and ask for what they want, and stay firm on boundaries that are best for their families. And, six months into the role, her team exceeded its sales goals. They are thriving with her at the helm as a leader.

Mike, an organizational culture consultant, elaborated on how the divide and conquer strategy works in his household. His wife is a successful doctor, and they have three children.

> "I like to think of our home as an organization where we each have certain duties. I call her marketing and HR. The kids go to her when somebody does something wrong. She sets up the social events, coordinates babysitters, and ensures the kids have birthday gifts for their friends, whereas my role is the CFO and Operations. I make sure the house is in order. When it comes to family trips, I am the captain of the minivan, and I handle the finances. We take on the roles that either are our strength or the other one isn't necessarily good at (or doesn't want). There are definitely times where it feels like one is doing more than the other. When we get like that, we voice our concerns because we realize as soon as we say it out loud, 'Oh yeah, you are doing things. I didn't see it.' We feel more empowered when it is a partnership."

Divide and conquer, like work-life balance, ebbs and flows. To Mike's point, there are some weeks when it feels like one is doing more than the other, yet when we take a step back and tally up roles and responsibilities, we often realize both partners are doing their fair share overall. Or, maybe the divide is lopsided, and that's what your family needs right now. Whether it is aligning roles with strengths together in the household, and supporting each other's careers equally, we create an environment where both careers have space to succeed, while showing our children what "good" looks like.

Have a Plan

This brings us to the third element of doing the fair share: having a plan. Male allies shared planning collaboratively with their partners at home, and for women leaders they work with that are mothers was vital to success. While gender socialization teaches women to plan early on, having input from male allies in our work-life strategy is important. Speak up and collaborate with your partner (or the women you support) on the right plan for the situation.

Mark is CEO of his own training company and partners with his wife to balance and plan family obligations alongside their companies. They both travel significantly. They have three children, one with a serious medical condition requiring frequent attention. As Mark shared,

"By no means do I claim to have this on lockdown, but my wife is a full-time professor. She's got a PhD in occupational therapy and teaches research at Creighton University. It's a very busy and demanding role in and of itself. She is a highly published academic author and puts in a lot of work, and she's respected on a global scale in her field. Plus, we have three kids. Plus we both have our own business. She has her own side hustle she works on. We're very busy from a professional standpoint, so this is where I think we get it really, really right, but it's where we really, really butt heads at the same time.

One of the places where this shows up for us: just this last week, she was in Philadelphia for seven days. We have a policy at our house that – because we have a child with Type 1 diabetes – one of us needs to be close to her throughout the week. Then we know she has adequate care and everything is taken care of. This last week, while my wife was gone for a conference, I didn't travel. In the first half of March, I was in Colombia for 13 days and she didn't travel."

As Mark outlines, they plan travel schedules in advance, and have policies to support the children and their well-being. When balance teeter totters, he is outsourcing and proactively delegating work in his business to free up time to balance other tasks at home. In fact, based on his experiences and challenges with work and life management, Mark is looking to extend his services in this area.

"I'm working to create a program just for young married men to help support these types of relationships. If you look at the model of the world from our parents' generation, you often had one decision maker – typically the dad or the husband.

Everybody might have a say but there's only one vote that really counts, right? Now, contrast that with our generation and you have two people in a household making budgetary decisions, making career decisions. Both are balancing all the priorities, and making child-rearing decisions. It's not necessarily just a one-sided equation any more. It's two powerful, likely educated people, getting to make these decisions together, and when you're the young male in the relationship you don't have a model of the world where that was true."

Generational differences bring with them implications on the partnership at home and at work. As Mark explains, the gender norms can limit men, too.

"Women tend to be more proactive about decision making, planning, child-rearing decisions, and so what a lot of young men do is compromise. They compromise to the point where they say, 'You handle it. I'll be fine.' The reality is: eventually, they're not fine. Then, we have resentment.

What I'd love to see more guys do – especially young guys – is to step up and collaboratively lead and communicate better with their spouses or with their significant others, so that we can avoid some of those resentment situations down the road. In my pursuit to support my wife and her career, I've done both. I've had the situation where I've compromised to the point where I didn't recognize myself, I didn't have the career I wanted. I sacrificed everything for her. Then we've gone the complete opposite direction where she felt she was sacrificing everything for me. Then we've also had the situation where we nailed it and we get what we want. What I love about being able to support her now is not that every day is perfect, but we're on a better track to create that blend of both of us having an amazing career and also having an amazing life together.

For example, in my coaching programs, I require my male coaching clients to plan one date night a week for 90 days. Not to wait for their wife to tell them where they want to go or anything like that; they can always adapt and adjust but they get to plan one date night, get the babysitter lined up if that's required, and make it happen."

Planning for activities like date night make a big impact on relationships. Being present for each other, and prioritizing and planning time to connect is key. When we stay in our prescribed gender roles, we limit ourselves, and risk sacrificing ourselves in the process. As I was writing this book, I had an interesting conversation with my husband, a strong male ally, about doing the fair share. We collaboratively debated how much of the household labor he and I did. I thought it was 50/50 – I do the grocery shopping, my own laundry (an outcome of a fabric softener dispute), child care duties (dependent on travel), and the finances. He stays home with our daughters, cooks, does the rest of the laundry, manages the yard work, and does light cleaning. We admittedly outsource hardcore cleaning which has a huge ROI for more family time and less stress. As we broke down our roles, I realized it was more like 60 him/40 me, yet he still argues 70 him/30 me. While the debate ensues, at this point in our family, this equation makes sense. That's likely to shift over time based on our family's needs, and that's a good thing. Do the math for your family, and compare notes. You will be surprised by the discussion, and may pick up on a thing or two you can do to help.

Your male allyship is paving the way for equality. The ordinary things you do to support women make an extraordinary impact.

Male Ally Action Steps

With the women in mind you want to support – knowing their stories and speaking up with them – it's now time to think about the fair share.

1. As a father yourself, or on behalf of fathers you know, how will you advocate "all in" parenting for everyone, equally?

2. As a partner yourself, or for the women you support as a male ally, how will you support dividing and conquering personally and professionally?

3. For the women you have chosen, how will you support the plan for their future success?

SECTION SIX:
WE ARE ONE

CONCLUSION

We need to multiply our male allies. Those featured in this book – and those you know – are not enough. We need more. Positive peer pressure works. Our call to action is for you to spread the word to other "potentials," on the fringe, who want to help support women (but may not know how). Share our strategies with them to enlist support – Heart, Story, Speak, and Work-Life.

For organizations looking to encourage male allyship, think about what you learned from the Wharton 22s. If you do not have a male ally group, form one. If your organization has a women's professional development group, invite men to participate. Organizations embracing male allies outperform those that do not. You are leaving money on the table if you are not facilitating male allyship. Becoming an ally is a journey. For regular doses of inspiration to keep you going, we also recommend following @betterallies on Twitter.

From our research, we found organizations with gender equality offer these best practices:

- A culture setting gender equality, inclusion, and diversity as a non-negotiable belief, and acts as a basis for "fit" with the organization.
- Goals to improve gender equality as a part of their strategic plan, with full transparency of statistics by gender for leadership roles and pay.
- Women's professional development groups that include male allies.
- Accountability for behaviors to support gender equality: heart, story, speak, and work-life.

If your organization is missing any of these best practices, Pivot Point is here to help. We have keynotes, workshops, and consulting services to foster gender equality in your organization.

We offer additional resources for platforms for positive change. Go to our website NextPivotPoint.com to download our mantra (see the Call to Action, next) and access the full interview audio from our featured experts.

While you're there, sign up for our bi-weekly newsletter and learn more about how we can support you with your action plan.

We're here to partner with your organization to facilitate male allyship!

CALL TO ACTION

Our goal in writing ONE was to create a call to action for more male allies to engage with women for gender equality, and for more women to engage with male allies for support (personally and professionally).

Men, if you believe in equal rights, it is time to step up. Channel the women you empathize, learn HERstories, speak up with them, and do the fair share. Be their mentor, sponsor, advocate, coach, advisor... whatever role that benefits them and is aligned with your strengths. Women, start the dialogue, share your story, speak up with men, and practice self-care.

We'll leave you with this Male Ally Challenge: share our mantra on social media using hashtags #maleallies, #genderequality, #femaleadvocacy, #ONE, and #heforshe.

OUR MANTRA

I believe in gender equality. I believe women and men, partnering together for gender equality, is what is best for all humans. By collaborating together, we will improve the lives of future women leaders and girls who will grow up in a world where anything is possible. My voice matters. I make choices every day supporting gender equality. We are all in this together. I commit to supporting male allyship. We are stronger together.

We are ONE.

ABOUT JULIE KRATZ
SPEAKER, TRAINER, & COACH

Julie Kratz is a highly-acclaimed leadership trainer who led teams and produced results in corporate America for nearly two decades. After experiencing her own career "pivot point," Julie developed a process to help women leaders create their winning career game plan. Focused on promoting gender equality in the workplace and encouraging women with their "what's next" moments, Julie is a frequent keynote speaker and executive coach. She holds an MBA from the Kelley School of Business at Indiana University and is a Certified Master Coach. Julie is the author of *Pivot Point: How to Build a Winning Career Game Plan* and *ONE: How Male Allies Support Women for Gender Equality*. Meet Julie at NextPivotPoint.com.